Nigel Rees is no stranger to cliché. He is **well known as a broadcaster** and as the **author of** several hundred **books.** A man of many parts, he has been **hospital porter, bodyguard, television producer and airline pilot. Awarded the OBE in 1979,** he is **married to an expert in English ceramic pottery** and **divides his time between homes in** Putney and Barnes. His enthusiasms are **music, beer, shove ha'penny and Morris dancing.** He is **currently writing a motion picture comedy** for 20th Century-Fox. **Nigel Rees is a Welsh octoroon.**

To my wife
without whom ...

Contents

Foreplay
On The Job
Winding Down
Boasting About It Afterwards
Slagging Off Your Partner Afterwards
If It Ends In Marriage

The Naming Of Books
The Writing Of The Biographical Note
The Writing Of The Blurb
Writing The Book
Writing Romantic Novels
  1 *The Hero*
  2 *The Heroine*
  3 *The Barbara Cartland Heroine*
  4 *The Asterisk*
  5 *The Clothes*
  6 *The Ultimate Plot Explanation*
Writing For Radio

With The Personal Approval of David Ogilvy

Contents

Introduction

You used to be taught never to touch clichés with a barge-pole. THE JOY OF CLICHÉS – as its title suggests – takes a different view. The author and his advisory committee believe that people should be *encouraged* to use such venerable, charming and off-the-tongue phrases.

Consequently, you will find here a complete user's guide, constructed in the most up-to-date scientific way, offering step-by-step instructions how to employ clichés in any number of everyday situations.

In addition, there are copious examples of the way clichés have been used by such distinguished speakers as HM the Queen, the Archbishop of Canterbury, Arthur Scargill and Little and Large, to name but a few. (Notice how successful these cliché-users are in public life. They obviously know what they are doing.)

Even if you are starting from scratch, you will soon be able to speak, write and read clichés as though to the manner born. This book unites the tentative, closet cliché-user with the card-carrying cliché-monger.

It should be pointed out, perhaps, that this book concerns itself, for the most part, with *verbal* clichés. The hawk-eyed reader will nevertheless detect one or two examples of cliché behaviour, cliché thought and cliché situations.

For ease of recognition, the clichés are mostly shown in **bold print**.

In no time at all, you will learn how to use clichés in the comfort of your own home and at the office, in pubs, in bed, on TV, in newspapers and on the cinema screen. In fact, THE JOY OF CLICHÉS tells you everything you wanted to know about them, but were afraid to ask.

Additionally, it is a book for all seasons and another best-seller from the author of the previous better one.

As has been truly said, 'Happiness is a worn cliché.'

After studying this guide you will surely agree that no home should be without one.

And now, dear reader, this is where the story really begins ...

NIGEL REES
Hotel Cipriani, Venice
May 1984

(dictated by Mr Rees
and signed in his absence)

Acknowledgements

I am grateful to Her Majesty the Queen who **graciously gave permission** for me to quote from one of her speeches and generally to extract the Princess Michael.

I am grateful to my employers for their patience and consideration towards a colleague whose **work has forced him to be more noticeable by his absence than his presence** during the writing of this book, not to mention their casting a blind eye on all the phone calls and photocopying I have done without telling anyone.

I am grateful to **long lists of people** whose names I am including in the hope that they will go out and buy a copy of the book for themselves.

I am grateful to the **copyright holders** of any documents I may have looked at for not witholding permission to reproduce them (perhaps because they did not know I was going to).

I am grateful to Nikki Norris for being at my side throughout the indexing of this volume. Readers will agree that the index **stands as a monument to her remarkable powers.**

At the typescript and proof stage I was **particularly helped by the rigorous scrutiny** of Lady Kintlesham. She also **told me an interesting anecdote about** her late husband. However, **I alone must accept responsibility for any errors.**

The care of Gloria Bust's research and the tirelessness of Jacky Lashmore's secretarial labours was **matched only by the patience of my wife.**

I am grateful to my editor, Alice Wood, for her **advice, patience and skill** in helping me to **deliver the book on time.**

Finally, I would like to thank clichés – **just for being there and for being such an enjoyable subject to write about.**

N.R.

(NB This is the sort of thing you should put at the beginning of a book. British authors are not expected to thank everybody. American authors are. They should start with the obstetrician who brought them into the world and carry on from there.)

NOTE
Throughout the book I have used the personal pronoun 'he'. **The only reason for this is that it is far less long-winded than writing 'he or she' every time.** 'Ladies' should not take offence. They may substitute 'she' if they feel so inclined.

In The Beginning

In the beginning was the Word, and the Word was taken up by lots of people and, in time, the Word became a Cliché.

That is the name of the game.

And, frankly, what it's all about.

At Your Mother's Knee, Or Thereabouts

Clichés are with us from the moment we are born. It is given to few of us to leap, fully literate, from our mother's womb and cry 'Let God be glorified,' as St Nicholas is supposed to have done. It is given to even fewer of us to announce 'Hello, good evening and welcome,' from a similar position.

So it is at our mother's knee, or thereabouts, that we first get introduced to the mystery of the spoken word. The first clichés we hear come from our parents' lips. It is one of the great ironies of life that those phrases we so loathe to hear as youngsters so readily spring from our own lips when, in time, we become fathers and, particularly, mothers.

I am thinking of such wondrous admonitions as:

it's time you settled down

This can be spoken to offspring of almost any age. It is especially effective when completed with:

and found a nice sensible job like your father's.

Especially suitable for use by the parents of teenage children is:

you treat this house like a hotel.

Care should be taken, however, lest offspring take such sayings as implying a literal call for their departure. Should this unfortunate event occur, or should the child commit offences which might attract the attention of the popular newspapers, it is essential for parents to practise saying:

we gave him/her everything ... where did we go wrong?

A little later during the brow-beating session/interview with the representative of the *News of the World*, it is equally appropriate and necessary to utter the sentiment:

it's his/her life

and:

he/she has got to live it the way he/she wants to.

Should some form of corrective punishment be called for – i.e. withdrawal of conjugal rights from your teenage daughter – it is best accompanied by the placatory:

it's for your own good.

Exercise

I hope that the foregoing phrases have a somewhat familiar ring to them. Even if they do not, say them over to yourself a number of times under your breath. A good time to do this is last thing at night before going to bed or while you are doing your early morning exercises.

Parents should seek the first possible opportunity to use clichés like these on their children. The response will be interesting to note.

Children should listen carefully and try to spot when their parents use the above phrases. It might be fun to award them points for the number of times they do so.

If nothing else, I hope this short introductory section will have alerted you to the existence of clichés in everyday life from a very tender age.

What Every Schoolboy Knows

All kinds of people have tended to say **as every schoolboy knows**. Jonathan Swift said it. Bishop Jeremy Taylor said it. Champion user without a doubt, however, was Thomas Babington Macaulay. He would say things like 'Every schoolboy knows who imprisoned Montezuma, and who strangled Atahualpa.'

Clearly it can't be wrong to say it. After all Macaulay did very well as a historian and was given a peerage for saying it. Nevertheless, the effect on schoolboys reading his historical essays has been pretty unnerving. I mean, do *you* (schoolboy or not) know who imprisoned Montezuma and who strangled Atahualpa? Search me.

The secret is, of course, that no one ever dared call the bluff of Macaulay or others who used this formulation. No one ever said, 'No we haven't a clue who imprisoned Montezuma or who strangled Atahualpa and what's more we are not frightfully interested.' And so they got away with it.

On balance, therefore, you are well advised to say it. You could get away with it, too.

Schoolteachers themselves should not say it – because, of course, they are aware that schoolboys know nothing at all. For this reason, schoolteachers have been apportioned two clichés of their own. No more than that, because they don't deserve it.

They complain a great deal about having to write end-of-term reports. But there is really no need to. They should simply put **could do better** whenever they can.

Teachers administering corporal punishment should, of course, invariably say to their victims:

you know, this hurts me more than it hurts you.

That is enough for teachers. They will have to fend for themselves from now on.

Naturally, you are only on the receiving end of such clichés as a child, but it is now time to consider the next stage in a child's development: using clichés yourself. Frankly, this is a big step. From having spent fifteen or eighteen years saying 'I want this' or 'I want that' you are now faced with the difficult task of entering the adult world where the use of clichés is a regular occurrence and a test of manhood.

No wonder you're coming out in acne.

But, fear not, relief is at hand . . .

Hail Cliché, Well-Met

I'd like you to meet Eric and Derek. They have something very important to impart to you. They are old chums, though they don't see very much of each other. When they do meet, however, they instantly pick up where they left off. The reason? They speak almost entirely in clichés. Keith and Steve are also past masters at coping with this kind of language. They will pop along in just a moment.

The Complete Conversation Guide
Students should study the following saloon bar conversation and commit the dialogue to memory. A good idea would be to get together with some chums and each take a role. When you are all word-perfect, you could go along to your local pub and perform the playlet. The real test is whether anyone notices or not. If they do not, you are well on the way to being a qualified cliché-speaker.

This dialogue may not work quite so well at the bus stop or in the supermarket, but students might care to experiment with the clichés and add their own where necessary. As every schoolboy knows, conversational clichés are very easy to acquire. Indeed, many students will have them at their fingertips already.

So, pull out the stops, plumb the depths and let's get down to brass tacks:

Scene: a saloon bar at the local hostelry. Eric is seated at the bar, communing with a g. & t. Derek enters, tripping the light fantastic, and spies his old friend:

DEREK: I say, Eric, old man, **long time no see!**
ERIC: Ah, Derek! Care to join me in **a little noggin?**
DEREK: Well, **since you twist my arm** …!

ERIC: What'll it be then?

DEREK: **Spot of the old vino**, if you don't mind.

ERIC: **Prefer the grape to the grain**, eh?

DEREK: Got to watch the **old ticker**.

ERIC (*confidentially*): I'll just **summon a lackey** ... **Mine host**! A glass of the **vino tinto** for the **walking wounded** here. And another g & t for me.

(*Mine Host goes about his business.*)

DEREK How's the **lovely lady wife**?

ERIC: The **better half**? **Positively blooming**. Mind you, spends far too much time at home watching the **one-eyed God** and smoking **coffin nails**. And how's your **little woman**?

DEREK: **Not getting any younger. Sic transit, narmean**[1]?

MINE HOST (*approaching with the drinks*): There we are, gentlemen.

DEREK: **What's the damage**?

MINE HOST: One pound fifty nine pee.

DEREK (*fishing in his pocket*): Let me just see if I can find the **wherewithal** ... there you are!

ERIC: Cheers! **Down the hatch!**

(*They drink. A busty blonde waddles past.*)

ERIC: Now, that's what I call a **sight for sore eyes!**

DEREK: I'm not so sure about her. She's **no chicken**, you know. Probably had more commercial travellers **than I've had hot dinners**.

ERIC: Perhaps you're right. (*Pause.*) That **your chariot** parked outside?

DEREK: The Sierra? Yes, **not a bad little bus. Plenty of gee-gees under the bonnet**.

ERIC: I had a *very* nasty experience at the weekend, Derek. I'd been up to the **Big Smoke** for a sales conference –

---

[1] This useful word was invented by A. Coren, wit and lover, and is, of course, a contraction of the more usual **know what I mean**? You can use either version.

DEREK: — well, its **better than work**, in'it?

ERIC: Now, come on Derek! Anyway, there I was, beetling along, foot on the **loud pedal**, when one of **our two-wheeled chums** came off a roundabout **like a bat out of hell**. All of a sudden it **looked like curtains** for **yours truly**.

DEREK: You thought, 'This is it!'

ERIC: **And how! Slammed on the anchor**, I did — and just missed chummy by a **coat of paint**. I'd nearly **run out of road**. Could have been **quite a tidy little prang**. Fortunately, **the boys in blue** weren't in sight. So I gave the **little prat** an **ear-full**. Told him he ought to **exercise the little grey cells a mite more** often. And left it at that.

DEREK Could have been the end of civilization **as we know it** for our Eric —

ERIC: — and **I don't mean maybe!**

(*Keith and Steve enter.*)

ERIC (*calling to the new arrivals*): Keith, still in the **land of the living**, I see! You know Derek, don't you?

KEITH: Of course (*shaking hands*). **Ill-met by moonlight** say I! This is Steve. Want to **wet your whistle** again?

ERIC: **I wouldn't say no.**

KEITH: Is that vino you're drinking, Eric? Another of the same? And Derek, **what's your poison?**

DEREK: I was thinking of **partaking of a little sustenance** in a short while, actually. Let me **do the honours.**

KEITH: No, no, have it on me. **Liberty Hall**, old boy.

DEREK: Well, another g. & t., please.

KEITH: Mine host, same again for these two gentlemen. Mine's a whisky — and yours, Steve?

STEVE: Don't mind me for a sec. Just going to **inspect the plumbing.**

DEREK (*knowingly*): **Nice work if you can get it!**

(*Steve goes to visit the* **smallest room.**)

ERIC: Well, where have you been **hiding your face?**

KEITH: Been on the **great silver bird**, haven't I?

ERIC: Anywhere exciting?

KEITH: Trade fair in Manila. Trouble is, **all the world and his wife** were there having a **well-earned rest** and I needed a foreign trip **like I need a hole in the head.** But you **can't win 'em all.** I mean, **if God had meant us to** enjoy ourselves at trade fairs he wouldn't have invented gyp in the tummy, now would he? Of which, **more anon.**

(*Steve returns from* **seeing a man about a dog.**)

STEVE: So, how's business? **Nose to the grindstone?**
ERIC: Pretty desperate. Still, as I always say, **it's bound to get worse before it gets better.**
KEITH: At least you're in **gainful employment** – which is more than can be said for my lad, Brian.
DEREK: Isn't he a graduate?
STEVE: Careful, Derek, **some of my best friends** are graduates!
DEREK: I dare say. I myself was less fortunate. I had to content myself with enrolling at the **University of Life** –
ERIC: – **School of Hard Knocks** –
DEREK: Be that as it may, the **vexed question** of Brian's future hangs heavy upon us. **Between these four walls** ...

(*At this moment, Mine Host produces all the drinks.*)

KEITH: Ah, thank you. I'll pay. (*He does so*) But, **back to our muttons.** Between these four walls, he's thinking of joining up with the boys in blue.
DEREK: Strewth! Well, **if you can't beat 'em, join 'em,** I suppose. Anyway, excuse me half a mo'. Got to use the **electric telephone** ... Mine host, have you a **book of words** for me to consult.
MINE HOST: The telephone directory?
DEREK: The very same. And could you **cast some light on the subject?**
MINE HOST: Sorry, do you need a lamp?
DEREK: Yes – I think I **could go so far as to say** 'yes'.

(*Mine Host supplies the directories and a lamp. Derek hunts for a number and finds it.*)

DEREK: I'll never remember this. I'll have to **set pen to paper**. (He does so.) 'Scuse me. It'll only take a tick.

(*He goes to the phone.*)

KEITH (*to Steve and Eric*): Well, how goes it?

STEVE: **Let's be honest**[2], meat pies aren't the **hottest thing since sliced bread**. But, **it's a living**.

ERIC: In meat pies are you? Someone who's in meat pies **can't be all bad**, say I.

KEITH: He's **not just a pretty face**, you know ...

STEVE (*offering cigarettes*): **Cancer stick**, anybody?

KEITH/ERIC: No, thanks.

DEREK (*returning*): Sorry, I've got to go. Time to go in search of a little something to eat, then **climb the wooden hill to Bedfordshire**.

ERIC: You mean, you're going home to Newport Pagnell?

DEREK: That's right ... **'God's own country'**!

ERIC: Well, **see you anon**.

DEREK: You two OK for transport? Sorry to break up the party. **Home James!**

(*Derek departs*)

STEVE: **To go** back to the wife **or not to go, that is the question** ...

KEITH: **Plus ça change** ...

ERIC: Do you fancy coming over for a cup of coffee or the **cup that cheers**?

KEITH: Anything **so long as it's wet and warm** –

STEVE: – and **refreshes the inner man**.

ERIC: **This is it.** Well, let's go then.

(*They bid adieu to Mine Host and fall through the door into the car park.*)

---

[2] This phrase appears by arrangement with B. Rix, charity organizer and ex-trouser-dropper. He used it six times within the space of one BBC TV *Breakfast Time* interview in 1983 and thus has made it his own.

Not Shakespeare, of course, but then it's not supposed to be. Look upon it just as a 'slice of life'. You won't find that kind of tuition on Linguaphone records. I wonder how those foreign students manage? That's something Professor Ernst Tlint, the chairman of the Cliché Advisory Council, is very hot on. I think it has something to do with a visit Ernst once paid to Basingstoke. He went into a pub and couldn't understand a word anyone was saying. 'They were talking English,' he wrote to me subsequently, 'and I could recognize the words, but I still could not understand what they were on about.'

Ah well, it was that Yugotour in reverse which set Ernst on the road to becoming, probably, the foremost foreign-language exponent of English clichés. A moment to compare with whoever it was first looking into Chapman's Homer.

It may interest readers to learn that one of Professor Tlint's party-tricks at social occasions (organized occasionally by the University of Zagreb) is to perform the above dialogue doing all five voices himself. The subtle way in which he delineates the characters, despite a noticeable Croatian accent, is a wonder to behold – or so his wife, Gleb, has assured me.

Three Great Facts To Drop Into Any Conversation

The relentless recycling of clichés so eloquently outlined in the dialogue above will suffice to keep most conversations on the boil for many a happy hour. However, if conversation shows signs of flagging, you can always rely on the following fascinating facts to revive it – not least because someone, somewhere will dispute their veracity:

1 The Victorians were so prudish they put antimacassars on piano legs.
2 Despite its prosperity, Sweden has the world's highest suicide rate.
3 Melbourne is the city with the second largest Greek population in the world.

Topics for Discussion

Then there are whole areas of thought which lend themselves to fruitful discussion. It is often said that television has killed the art of conversation stone dead (which might be an interesting topic for discussion in itself). I thought it would be useful, however, at this point, to suggest just a few areas around which the keen cliché-user might profitably employ his verbal techniques. They are, in no particular order:

1 **The commercialization of Christmas.**
2 **Christmas isn't what it used to be.**
3 **Fings in general ain't what they used to be.**
4 **Blood sports.**
5 **Deprived inner city areas.**
6 **Mid-life crises.**
7 **Last night's television.**
8 **Where shall we stop the car for our picnic?**

A confident use of clichés in the context of these topics should signal to the user that he or she is now well-qualified as far as everyday conversation is concerned. The next step is to embrace clichés in more specialized areas.

A Young Person's Guide

One of the difficulties in preparing a book of this kind is that clichés are constantly changing, not only in terms of what is or what is not a cliché at any particular moment but in terms of different age groups' perceptions. Today's cliché is yesterday's innovation or tomorrow's delightful archaism. It is quite likely, also, that young people of today would find it hard to conduct any of the dialogue exercises above with a straight face.

Broughton Poggs OBE, one of the members of the CAC (Cliché Advisory Council) most closely in touch with young people, has therefore come up with what he terms a 'converter kit'. This enables the punk or glue-sniffing youngster of today to converse in clichés without having to use some of the venerable phrases so beloved of the likes of Eric and Derek.

I believe that Broughton is thinking of writing his own guide-book to explain this 'converter-kit' more fully than I can do. There is only room here for me to give a brief indication of how it works. He lent me the prototype for a weekend recently (it works rather like a home computer) and I spent many happy hours trying to understand the instructions.

Basically, the conversation in the local hostelry stands as the model for all cliché conversations. What varies is the precise phrases used. (The props are also different — bondage gear instead of Marks and Spencer suits, funny cigarettes in place of g. and t.'s, for example.) You feed in a venerable cliché like 'All the world and his wife' at one end and out pops the more contemporary phrase at the other.

Well, that's the theory. I tried it out and append my findings:

For 'care to join me in a little noggin?', substitute:
> 'I don't know whether you're **in touch with my feelings**.'

For 'since you twist my arm', substitute:
> 'the **vibes are good**.'

For 'that your chariot parked outside?', substitute:
> 'how's your **karma**?'

For 'plus ça change', substitute:
> 'I am glad you are **sharing an insight** with me.'

For 'and I don't mean maybe', substitute:
> '**answer-wise**.'

For 'if you can't beat 'em, join 'em', substitute:
> 'I really **relate** to it, y'know.'

For 'I think I could go so far as to say', substitute:
> 'I feel I'm having a **meaningful dialogue**.'

For 'like I need a hole in the head', substitute:
> 'I've found my **personal space**.'

For 'got to watch the old ticker', substitute:
> 'I'm just being **laid back** about it.'

For 'probably had more commercial travellers than I've

had hot dinners', substitute:

　'she's not **into commitment**.'

For 'more anon', substitute:

　'that's in a different **time-frame**.'

For 'positively blooming', substitute:

　'we **interact**.'

For 'I wouldn't say no', substitute:

　'let's **conceptualize**.'

For 'just going to inspect the plumbing', substitute:

　'I think we should **go with the flow**.'

I think this is how it is supposed to work. Forgive me if I'm wrong. I'm rather hoping that Broughton will come up with a simpler version of the kit very soon.

Nobs Oblige

Some have clichés thrust upon them, some are born to clichés. Should you happen to have been born an aristocrat, there are one and a half to two clichés, tried and tested for your exclusive use:

Men And Horses I Have Known

Firstly, when challenged with the fact that you have inherited vast wealth which you have done nothing to earn, you should reply:

> 'But, of course, all this (*gesturing*) doesn't really belong to me. I see myself as more of a **caretaker for my descendants.**'

Secondly, when asked what advantage you find in having a title, you should on no account think of anything original to say. The required response is:

> 'I don't think the title helps me at all. I think the only advantage of being a Duke is that **it does help in a crowded restaurant when you're trying to get a table.**'

Both these responses were admirably used by Gerald Grosvenor, 6th Duke of Westminster, when interviewed on BBC TV's *Aristocrats*, in November 1983. One gathered that the Duke had undergone special TV training in order to come across positively. He certainly did.

Well done, Your Grace!

The Show Must Go On

So You Want To Be In Show Business?
Then if **you've got the talent, you'll find a way** ... That is the first show business cliché.

Agents and impresarios may try to put you off with **Don't call us ... we'll call you**. You will suffer a bit and play a few duff parts. This, however, is all good material for the interviews you will have to give in due course and for the autobiography you must surely one day write.

Then you will undergo the second big showbiz cliché – which is **to be discovered**. Even if this process is nothing like the way they show it in the movies, you can always dress it up with hindsight.

Eventually the star will break a leg on opening night and you will obey the instruction to **go out there and enjoy yourself**. Only a matter of moments after this you will come back a great big star, with your name in lights.

You will take part in a **New Revue**. No one has ever discovered an 'old revue' so this will have to do. Your director implores: **Let's see it in the eyes** and, on the first night, invites you to **break a leg, old thing!** You get wonderful notices – or, at least, they are wonderful when you have chiselled out phrases like:

the audience roared!
laugh-a-minute
this one will run and run
see it!

One day it will be necessary to put up notices saying **Must Close** (which makes it sound as though you'd just *love* to keep on doing it but they won't let you). Meanwhile, you are 'Held over for 7th Great Week **by public demand**' (which simply means the management are hoping to screw another week out of it and you).

You may find you are hating every moment, you too by now have a broken leg, your sinuses are playing up, your marriage has just hit the rocks, but **the show must go on** for **there's no business like show business**.

You take on cabaret engagements and declare – at least once every performance – **there's so much love in this room** ...

Accepting Awards

Then come the big awards. In the days when you were accepting the one for The Most Struggling Newcomer, you could get away with saying things like:

I'm speechless ...

or:

I've left my ad-libs on my seat ...

but now you are a star you have to give it all you've got. Not all of us can turn in a glittering acceptance speech to rank with those of Lord Olivier or Sir Richard Attenborough. Yet we can try. And we can cry. Remember:

this is the proudest moment of my life ...

    (nobody minds if you use this three years running)

I'd like to thank all the people behind the scenes ...

    (name them all)

I'd like to thank (*name the director/producer*) **for having so much faith in me** ...

    (explain in the minutest detail why)

it won't change my life ...

    (*how true*)

this award isn't for me, it's for ...

    (name all these people, too. The list should include your mother.)

In no time at all, you will find you are not just a star but someone **respected by his fellow artistes**.

Can there be anything else for you to learn?

Well, yes.

The Complete Star Interview

To be a success in show business these days it is just not enough to have talent or a nice pair of legs. You have to go on the hype trail and answer idiot questions from showbiz journalists and TV chat show hosts. The questions *they* ask are covered in the section of this book dealing with radio and television. Read on, however, for advice on the answers *you* should give.

(Miss World contestants should not attempt more than two questions. In fact, it would be better if they just concentrated on question 10 – which should be avoided by everyone else.)

Q1 Why are you in London at the moment?
A **Oh, I love it here. Everyone is so friendly!**
   (NB Do *not* say 'I'm here to plug my latest picture,' even if you're talking to G. Hunniford or R. Harty.)

Q2 What are your feelings about California?
A **I hate California. That's why I've come to London – to find my own space.**

Q3 What do you hope to do while you're over here?
A **Oh, I wanna see Buckingham Palace** (that'd be a real thrill), **the Tower of London, and those cute little old antique shops in the Portobello Road.**

Q4 What are your first reactions to London?
A **I love your British fish and chips and I think your policemen are wonderful.**
   (This response may seem naïve in the light of recent British police behaviour but should still be given. K. Wayborn, Swedish crumpet and *Octopussy* star, told a *Guardian* reporter (4 June 1983): 'They [British policemen] are so wonderful. They make you feel so secure.')

Q5 What are your relations with (*name of any other well-known film star*) since you split up?
A Oh, I think we can say **we are having a truly loving separation. Of course, it's a heartache.** (*Pause*) But we are looking upon it as **a growing experience.**
   (This answer is modelled on the inspirational attitudes of

D. and T. Shire who actually experienced 'a very loving separation' in Hollywood. Said she: 'We're going to rotate the house and we even rotate the car. We've been separated for four months and it's a growing experience.')

Q6 What about your new film? Who will it appeal to?
A Oh, **children of all ages, from 9 to 90.**

Q7 How did you first turn to comedy?
A At school I was always being bullied. But **I found that if I made people laugh they left me alone.**

Q8 Which do you prefer – working in films or the theatre?
A Oh, **I love them both.** They are totally separate mediums. **I like to do both** (as much as I can).

Q9 Is there any nudity in this film (*or* Do you take your clothes off?)
A Yes, but **it's absolutely vital both to the character and to the integrity of the script.**
  (My thanks to G. Jackson, Oscar-winner and former sales person in Boots the Chemist, for her valuable advice in preparing this response. She has also been talking, it seems, to Lord Delfont who is quoted by Hunter Davies in *The Grades* (Weidenfeld & Nicolson, 1981), as saying: 'I do allow four-letter words and nudity in my films, if they are in the right context, if it has integrity.' Alternatives are: **I don't mind if it's relevant to the script** or **if it's done in a meaningful way.** Best to avoid **yes, but it's all done in the best possible taste** for the time being.)

Q10 What are you going to do with the prize money if you win?
A **I am going to buy a kidney machine for my dying mother.**

If asked a question not listed above, answer:
A **Oh no, I think there's too much reality in the world today, don't you?**
  That'll soon put a stop to their silly questions.

It is not given to all of us to become showbiz stars and to be on the receiving end of such inquiries. On the other hand, we may have to meet such stars from time to time. And so:

Advice To Hangers-On, Stage-Door Johnnies And Others Who May Have To Go Backstage After A Performance

If you meet a performer after the show it is not considered adequate to say **darling, you were marvellous!** You may even find *that* hard to say if you did not actually enjoy the show. Consider, therefore, some of the following alternatives:

1 **you old rogue!**
   (notice how neatly this sidesteps a comment on the performance)
2 **you've done it again!**
   (exactly what you've done is nicely left unstated)
3 **what a performance!**
   (beautifully ambiguous)
4 **you gave the performance we have come to expect from you!**
   (I once had to write a review of a play in which I had appeared. I considered that 'Rees gave the performance we have come to expect from him' could be interpreted as people wished)
5 *you* **couldn't have been better!**
   (even if that's not saying much)
6 **good is not the word!**
   (ah, but what is the word?)
7 **I don't care what anybody says — *I* thought you were marvellous!**

Sex Rears Its Ugly Head

The English language is rich in words. There are, say, ten words for almost every human activity you might care to name. For one human activity in particular, however, there are many more than ten words. And some of them have more than four letters. You may find the following expressions useful in the comfort of your own bed:

The Initial Approach

Most sexual clichés fall into the first phase of the seduction process as this is when most of the talking is done – what we sexologists call 'the Chat Up' stage. It is given to few people to come up with an original sexual advance, so most of us have to rely on the time-honoured selection printed here below. It is striking just how many Chat Up clichés there are. On the advice of Council member Christopher Ferrat, who knows about these things, I have segregated the lines between male and female chatters-up. The reader will be able to judge the appropriateness of this manoeuvre from his or her own experience:

He: **do you come here often?**
  (only very confident or middle-aged female cliché-users should attempt the reply: **only in the mating season.**)
He: **if you won't sleep with me, it won't go down**
  (there have been numerous recorded instances of this ingenious approach, particularly among Oxford undergraduates of the early 1960s. It is best not tried on women with a medical background as they might question the basis of the claim.)

He/She: **you really turn me on**
(well, if you must ...)

He: **my wife doesn't understand me**
(one of the all-time greats, this one.)

when are you going to finish off that dress?
(addressed to woman with skimpy décolletage.
T. Jones, Welsh superstar and trouser-torturer,
has gone so far as to include this in his act. I
personally witnessed him trying it on a member
of the audience at Caesar's Palace, Las Vegas,
in May 1972. Whether it led to the promised
consummation, history does not record.)

He: **you shouldn't wear those thigh boots if you don't
mean it**
(naturally.)

She: **hello, sailor**
(you'll have to decide for yourself whether you
are buying or selling.)

He: **hello, sailor**
(something for every taste.)

She: **you've got what it takes**
(yes, people really do say this sort of thing.)

He/She: **help me make it through the night**
(I think this may be a line from a song. Best
avoided if you are not sure.)

He: **voulez-vous couchez avec moi, ce soir?**
(a bit bold this one, but I suppose there are some
women who would need a dictionary to deal
with it.)

She: **if you want anything, just whistle**
(an allusion to a film with Lauren Bacall and
Humphrey Bogart in it. Probably best left to
those who are seeking love in their maturer
years.)

She: **would you like to come up for a cup of coffee?**
(this is what Mae West *meant* to say but, as is
well known, never did. Should not be used
lightly.)

He: **are there any more at home like you?**
(T. Jones, at it again.)

He: **I could help get you into films**
(for some reason largely confined to use by greasy wops. In line for refurbishing, surely?)

He: **that's my favourite girl's name**
(I once had a neighbour who was a Polish Count – at least, I think that's what he said. He would always begin his chat-ups by asking the girl her name. Whatever she replied – Cathy, Gladys, Gleb – he would make this response. I'm told it sometimes worked.)

He: **where have you been all my life till now?**
(all right, if you think you can manage it.)

He: **we've run out of petrol/gas**
(I had to include this.)

He: **I like your mind**
(Jacky Lashmore, my secretary, always responds to this approach, for some reason.)

He: **no, it won't make you drunk, honest**
(once aboard the lugger and she's mine ...)

He: **what's a nice girl like you doing in a place like this?**
(I don't know whether people really say this sort of thing any more. Do they?)

He: **just as soon as I can I'm going to leave my wife and marry you**
(a former British Cabinet minister swears by this one.)

He: **your place or mine?**
(the pick of the bunch, in my opinion. Straightforward, practical, but not too direct.)

Offers From A Third Party

do you want to meet my sister?
(rather Mediterranean, this approach. Certainly very un-British. Don't be disappointed if you fail to detect a family resemblance.)

Rejecting Advances

Oddly enough, quite a lot of rejection still goes on – even despite the careful use of the above lines. You may even feel the need to do a spot of rejecting yourself if a potential partner proves unsuitable. Take care to choose the right excuse, otherwise it could end in tears. I asked Christopher Ferrat to think of some cliché lines for men in this area but he has failed to deliver. Surely this can't be because men never reject advances? As a temporary measure, men are advised to use one of the following – though I would be the first to admit that some of them are unsatisfactory:

She: **I've got a headache**

She: **I didn't think you were like that, Nigel**

She: **what happened to all the nice young men?**
(these last two can be run together, as I know to my cost.)

She: **all you men want is One Thing**

She: **you only want me for my body**
(my secretary, Jacky Lashmore, speaks highly of this one.)

She: **I've just had my hair done**
(clearly, this is not one that men can use, unless they are E. John or J. Young.)

She: **I don't want to ruin a perfect evening**
(even if this response will ruin *his*.)

She: **I'm having my period**
(naff, but there you are.)

Foreplay

Let us assume, for the sake of argument, that the Initial Approach has worked and that Rejecting Advances has not (otherwise we won't be here all night.) Now we can get on with the job. I'm afraid men are pretty negligent in this area so there are no male foreplay clichés.

She: **ah, I see sex has reared its ugly head**
(what a curious expression this is! Why is it
always ugly? I have no idea. Of course, you
don't have to be in bed to say this. In fact, you
are much more likely to be saying it at meetings
of the Women's Institute or on *Woman's Hour*.)

She: **John told me you were a very nice person but he
didn't tell me about *that!***
(careful!)

On The Job

He: **does it hurt when I do that ...?**
She: **stop ... stop!**

Winding Down

The Post-Coital Conversation can be cliché-free, if you like.
There really is no pressure on you to say anything if you
don't want to. However, if it is the first time together for you
both and if the seduction was a long, drawn-out one,
remember:

She: **I didn't want you to think I was an easy lay.**

Boasting About It Afterwards

This is what it's all about, really. There is no need to spare
your partner's feelings. You can exaggerate shamelessly.
Just hope that nothing of what you say gets fed back to
your partner:

He: **give her half a bottle of retsina, two olives and she's
anybody's ...**
She: **he's hung like a horse, my dear!**
He: **sleep, old chap? I had to get out of bed to go to sleep**
She: **he can leave his boots under my bed anytime**
(this was once said to me by a small lady of
Iranian extraction regarding Robert Redford.
Whether she really had had the pleasure is a

question that could be debated as long as there
are hedgehogs in Hampstead.)
She: **she's a very attractive woman, and there's nothing
funny about me**

Slagging Off Your Partner Afterwards

The other side to the above coin. A limited range of clichés
is available and if you really must, you really must:

He: **she's studied more ceilings than I've had hot dinners**
(Nikki Norris is threatening to walk out on the
Index if I include this one.)

He: **she wears her cunt on her sleeve**
(Jacky Lashmore is only typing this under
protest, so she tells me.)

He: **they all look the same in the dark**
(Gloria Bust wants it to be known that she
didn't research *this* entry.)

He: **you don't look at the fireplace when you're poking
the fire**
(Help! I've got a revolt on my hands.)

If It Ends In Marriage

Ah, that's better. The team is back together again. If all the
foregoing material is put into practice then the result could
be that you will end up getting married. Or, indeed,
unmarried. If the former, people will tell you:

you are **embarking on the Great Adventure**
that **the First Five Years Are The Hardest**
you are **making an honest woman of her**
that **our loss is....'s gain**.

Getting Married is perhaps the major situational cliché,
particularly at the end of a work of fiction. In real life, when
asked why you got married, you will hear yourself lamely
replying:

it seemed like a good idea at the time ...

Doctor,
I Think I'm Expecting A
Cliché

There is one main medical cliché and that is:

if in doubt, consult your GP

– which is odd because one of the great myths of the twentieth century is that GPs actually know anything. To be fair, though, they do know one thing. They know what to give you to produce side-effects which they then don't know what to do about.

In The Surgery

Doctors say things like:

well, well, Mrs———, and what seems to be the trouble?

(*And Out Again Within Two Minutes*)

My doctor recommends gargling with whisky for most ailments. So I have taken to staying at home and drinking whisky without consulting him.

In the Dentist's Chair

I have a great respect for dentists, on the other hand – despite one who tried to drill my teeth while shaking from drugs taken for his alcohol problem. It is just that dentists concentrate on one part of the body and seem to know what they are doing most of the time.

Their favourite line:

does it hurt when I do that ...?

This should not be mistaken for a similar cliché in the

previous chapter. Unless, of course, you like that sort of thing. There's a name for people like you.

And, finally:

just a little rinse, please ...

Clitch-Clitch-Clitch

'Politics,' as the saying goes, 'is the art of the possible.' It is also the art of the cliché. The Houses of Parliament are Britain's foremost arena for the use of clichés and I am happy at this juncture to invoke the name of a man who served with distinction in both the Commons and the Lords.

David Kintlesham was a conscientious backbench Tory MP for more than twenty-five years. His Private Member's Bill to control the indiscriminate import of Taiwanese lentils (a measure eventually incorporated in the Trade and Industries Act 1957) stands as his monument. Created a Life Peer in 1971, when his seat was required for redistribution purposes, he went on to contribute wisely to debates in the Lords, particularly on agricultural matters.

On his death in 1979, Daphne Kintlesham asked me if I would inspect her husband's papers – a task I fell to with alacrity. These papers are now available to scholars and anyone else who might be interested at Ealing Public Library (Hanger Lane branch).

Perhaps the chief jewel in the collection is the original manuscript of David Kintlesham's House of Commons speech on the occasion of the landing by Metropolitan policemen in Anguilla (1969). Comparison between the text as it was delivered and as it is recorded in *Hansard* (Vol. cxxiv, cols. 123-31) shows little discrepancy.

The aspiring politician would do well to study it closely and, if possible, commit the speech to memory, because it contains – to a remarkable degree – all the stylistic phraseology that he could possibly need, regardless of political party, of the subject on which he is supposed to be speaking, or of the occasion.

Ernest Bevin, Labour's Foreign Secretary after the Second World War, once described a speech by Anthony Eden as 'Clitch after clitch after clitch'. And Winston Churchill once had to deny he had ever said about an Eden speech that it 'contained every cliché known to man except "Prepare to meet thy God" and "Please adjust your dress before leaving".'

I know for a fact that the deliverer of the following speech – David Kintlesham – would have been proud to have had such things said about his work (commentary can be found at the conclusion):

David Kintlesham's Celebrated Speech:
'My friends(1),

'We meet today in a grave situation which **concerns us all** – indeed, in a situation unparalleled in this country's long history and one that we can only **view with alarm**.

'**But before dealing with that, let me just say this**(2) ... because I want to **nail the lie**, once and for all. **The Labour Government would be failing in its duty if it failed to** do anything about it.

'As I go **up and down the country**, I am frequently asked what *is* the Government going to do about it? – and not only by members of the Conservative Party but by what Labour supporters tend to refer to as **that great movement of theirs**(3).

'At the **grass roots**, and **in a caring society**, we must not tolerate those forces which seek to **drive a coach and horses**(4) through any policy of this kind. The consequence of such an approach would, frankly, be a decline in the **quality of life**.

'**The message of Anguilla**(5) is that the great majority of voters believe the time has come for the people of the **free world** to **stand shoulder to shoulder** in order to resist a **bloodstained tyranny** and to do so with their **gloves off**.

'**I want to make it perfectly clear**(6) precisely where I stand on this issue. The Government must **explore every avenue** and **leave no stone unturned** in its search for a solution. There is a **wind of change**(7) blowing through our **kith and kin**(8) which I profoundly believe will lead us to those **broad, sunlit uplands**(9) of which **that great Parliamentarian, Winston Churchill**, used to speak.

(And – let me say – most of the others are **dwarves and pygmies beside him.**)

'**Having said that**(10), I believe to be quite honest with you – that it is time for us to **stand up and be counted** and to **point with pride** towards it. **The spirit of Anguilla**(11) will surely carry us through.

'**When all is said and done**, there is **plenty of work about if you look for it**, and I believe there is a solution which will benefit **each and every one of us**(12). If we do not tackle the problem and seek a **just and lasting**(13) solution, we shall never see the **light at the end of the tunnel**(14) which I believe, profoundly, to be there.

'**Let me finish**(15) by asking you – and the **people of this country**(16) – to **face the future before us**, to ignore the merchants of **gloom and doom** and to take part with me in a **great debate** with the **rank and file**.

'**Mussolini may have made the trains run on time**, but – let's face it – **in the last analysis** it **all comes down to this ...**'

Notes On The Above

1 '*My friends*': technically, D. Kintlesham was in error addressing the House of Commons in this fashion but he so liked the phrase and believed in it so strongly that even the *Hansard* writers, I note, have not bothered to correct him.

2 '*before dealing with that, let me say just this*': the wise politician always uses this phrase when being interviewed on television in order to slip in a statement which he has learned off by heart and which has nothing to do with the interviewer's question. If used carefully, it can lead to the interviewer moving on to the second question without having obtained an answer to his first.

Never say 'and now let me answer your question'. That will only throw the interviewer who will have forgotten what it was. Here, D. Kintlesham is using the formula with the instinctive grace for which he was renowned.

3 *'that great movement of theirs'*: a sobriquet which belongs, as of right, to the Labour Party – in the form 'This Great Movement of Ours'. A delicious example of D. Kintlesham's sense of irony. Often abbreviated to 'THIGMOU' by Labour supporters. However, as the Labour Party can no longer be called great and shows no discernible sign of movement these days, the expression can be used to describe any other group which the speaker aspires to flatter.

4 *'drive a coach and horses'*: extra points for using this venerable and in no way dated metaphor. Be grateful to Sir S. Rice (1637-1715) who used it as long ago as when he did. A Roman Catholic Chief Baron of the Exchequer, Sir S. would use the courts in Dublin to get his own back on the Act of Settlement. 'I will drive a coach and six through the Act of Settlement,' he used to say.

From *The Times* (22 October 1983): 'Labour lawyers argued that Mr Justice Mervyn Davies had "driven a coach and horses" through Conservative legislation designed to limit the scope of trade disputes and outlaw political strikes, by refusing to ban the "blacking" of Mercury.'

5 *'The Message of——'*: insert here the name of any bye-election your party has just won or any other recent political excursion e.g. Orpington, Darlington, Crosby, Dunkirk, Chappaquiddick etc: ' "The S.D.P. bubble has burst," crowed Fallon. "That is the message of Darlington." ' (*Time*, 4 April 1983)

6 *'I want to make it perfectly clear'*: W. Whitelaw, Conservative politician and good chap, subsequently made this phrase his own, subtly varying it according to mood – e.g. 'I *have* made it perfectly clear' – or extending it with fitting self-justification, i.e. 'I want to make it perfectly clear – and it is only fitting and right, and right and fitting, and proper, so to do.' (Critics who suggest that, on the contrary, the phrase does not lead to greater clarity, may safely be ignored.)

7 '*wind of change*': H. Macmillan, Conservative Prime Minister and G.O.M., used this trope with great effect when addressing the South African Parliament in 1960. He called one volume of his memoirs *Winds of Change*. Well done!

8 '*kith and kin*': difficult to slip in, this one. However, I. Smith, Rhodesian rebel and former pilot, did well with it in about 1965. His pronunciation – 'keeth and keen' – should be attempted only by the more confident student.

9 '*broad, sunlit uplands*': W. Churchill was always on about these and presumably he has now found them, rather like the light at the end of the tunnel.

10 '*having said that*': unjustifiably criticized by some on the grounds that it usually means you have not said anything at all or are forcing a link between paragraphs. Such strictures are best ignored.

11 '*The spirit of*——': like 'the message of——' this is a highly versatile cliché. The 'Spirit of '76' came into use following the American Revolution. D. Eisenhower, US President and golfer, was very fond of the form, several times speaking in 1955 of the 'Spirit of Geneva' (not to be confused with Evian water). D. Eisenhower next conjured up the 'Spirit of Camp David' in 1959.

M. Foot, Labour politician and dog-walker, triumphantly restored the phrase to use in May 1983 and scored a double hit when he said, following a bye-election victory, that Labour would 'Get the spirit of Darlington up and down the country'. What a pity the Darlington win was reversed at the General Election the following month and that Mr Foot relinquished the party leadership! He could have used the phrase again.

12 '*each and every one of us*': strictly speaking this should only be attempted by American politicians – but it may be catching on elsewhere. Note especially H. Washington's words when he became Mayor of Chicago in May 1983: 'I'm a peacemaker who reaches out to each and every one of you.'

13 '*just and lasting*': comes with the A. Lincoln Seal of Approval. He talked of a 'just and lasting peace' in his

Second Inaugural address, referring to the end of the American Civil War.

14 *'light at the end of the tunnel'*: you cannot call yourself a politician if you do not say this. S. Baldwin saw one in 1929, N. Chamberlain in 1937, P. Reynaud in 1940, W. Churchill in 1941, J.F. Kennedy in 1962, and there was always light at the end of the tunnel during the Vietnam War. Perhaps there still is. Don't spoil it by adding that the light at the end of the tunnel is only the light of an oncoming train.

15 *'Let me finish'*: a better use is when being interviewed by irritating broadcasters such as Sir R. Day. Say 'Let me finish what I was saying' when he interrupts you with a supplementary question. Then go on and say something completely new and unconnected with whatever it was you *were* saying!

16 *'people of this country'*: again, W. Whitelaw shows us how to use this excellent phrase – and how to bury it and lift his argument at one and the same time. Following the end of the siege at the Iranian embassy in London (May 1980), he commented: 'The operation, and I think the people of this country and many in the world will think so too, was an outstanding success.' You can say that again, Willie!

The Art Of Resignation In Politics

Should you find that the above speech works for you and you are invited to join the Government (something which, alas, never happened to David Kintlesham) it may subsequently occur that you have to resign. In this case there are certain well-tried formulae for you to use.

If the Prime Minister is giving you the boot, a short letter is all that is required of you, but it should contain the following phrases:

'Dear Prime Minister:

'When we talked earlier today, you asked me if I would **put my job at your disposal**. This I am, of course, **most happy to do**.

'I shall always be grateful for having had the honour of working with you and serving this government.

'Yours sincerely,
'Eric'

If you are not leaving under a cloud you can afford to ramble on a bit and summarize all your achievements, such as they have been, in office. This is a useful bit of PR and could lead to your getting a few company directorships – which wouldn't go amiss. You may also drop in the line: 'I am very grateful to you for the many personal kindnesses you have shown me.' Even if this only means that the Prime Minister once let you use the payphone in the hallway of No. 10, it suggests a level of intimacy that might impress others.

If, on the other hand, you have been caught *in flagrante* with your secretary or the Chief Whip, or both, it is vital that you issue a Personal Statement. This should make two things perfectly clear: 1) you **deeply regret any embarrass-ment that may have been caused** to the Government and to your family and friends, and 2) your **wife and family are standing by** you. In fact, to get it absolutely right, your wife and family should be standing by you while you write the statement. You may add: 'My own feelings may be imagined.' (And that is the best way to leave them.)

If you are a Prime Minister you should always reply in the following way:

'Dear Eric,

'You made it clear to me some time ago that your office was at my disposal whenever the circumstances became desirable. For private and family reasons you were beginning to feel the burdens of office too heavy. It was characteristic of you to write in this way.

'I am sure you realize the need in the present situation for a broad reconstruction of the Government with a view to the future, and I am grateful to you for facilitating this.'

If Eric has been a naughty boy, you should be brief but not curt and add:

> 'Your decision **accords with the best traditions of British public life.**'

Hear, hear!

Ongoing Industrial Action

To trade union leaders, the cliché comes as a gift from the gods, to coin a phrase. I mean, what else can you say when nobbled by TV and newspaper reporters on the doorstep before you have even had a chance of referring matters to your Executive Committee?

An A-Z Of Union-Speak

It is important for every trade unionist – whether on the shop floor or in the Executive Committee or at Congress House – to use clichés at every opportunity. I believe it is especially important for members of the two unions to which I myself belong – the National Union of Journalists and the British Actors' Equity Association – to assist their brothers and sisters in doing this. Journalists should help with the choice of words, actors with the requisite delivery. It is difficult to describe this delivery on the printed page. If readers are unfamiliar with the likes of Mr Len Murray, they should acquire a heavy cold instead. On no account should readers attempt the delivery of Mr Clive Jenkins. One is quite enough.

Listed below, you will find thirty key words in the trade union vocabulary. I have tried to explain what each one means and how to use it. I have also included one or two examples of their use. In order to show how attractive Union-Speak can be to the general audience, the examples are drawn in some cases from people you may never have thought of as trade unionists!

action, industrial: one of the subtlest terms in the rule book. It does, of course, mean quite the reverse of what it pretends to mean – as in, 'It is to be hoped that tomorrow's Day of Action, incorporating industrial action in all key sectors of industry, will bring the whole country to a grinding halt.'

age, in this day and: 'In this day and age, I should have thought it was perfectly possible for management and unions to get together round a table and thrash these problems out like grown men, but apparently not ... etc.'

analysis, in the last: I think I am correct in including this one under Union-Speak but by doing so I might just have given rise to a demarcation dispute involving the Amalgamated Society of Political Speechwriters (ASPS) and the Federation of Broadcasting Interviewers (FBI).

bargaining, free collective: so much better than 'negotiations' as it includes a nice hint of 'free for all'.

call, not what you'd: an easy way into unpleasant statements – as in, 'Not what you'd call a fruitful meeting and it would be wrong of me to raise any false hopes with regard to the settling of this unnecessary dispute which has caused untold and completely unnecessary suffering to thousands of hospital patients following the management's totally unjustified ... etc, etc.'

cards, on the: 'A settlement to the dispute is on the cards ...'

day, at the end of the: Anthony Howard, distinguished journalist and editor, interviewing some BBC big-wig in *Radio Times*, March 1982, asked, 'At the end of the day one individual surely has to take responsibility, even if it has to be after the transmission has gone out?' As far as I can remember he was not talking about the TV Epilogue. (You will find another distinguished example in the chapter MY CLICHE AND I. See also OUR REPORTER ...)

democratically-elected: union officials are, and you should never lose an opportunity to remind people in management of this because they aren't, of course.

duck, lame: especially when combined with 'situation' (see below).

escalation (or de-): about the one good thing that came out of the Vietnam war, in actual fact.

fact, in actual: as above.

Genghis Khan, well to the right of: indispensable, this one. Arthur Scargill, President of the National Union of Mineworkers, told John Mortimer in the *Sunday Times* (10 January 1982), 'Of course, in those days, the union leaders were well to the right of Genghis Khan.'

inconvenience, sorry for any ... caused: 'We are of course very sorry for any inconvenience that may occur to the public, but ...' This cleverly enables you to disrupt public services, make your point and apologize at the same time. If there were no inconvenience you would not be able to make your point and you would not have anything to apologize for.

Compare the standard form of British Rail apology, so splendidly performed by members of the NUR and ASLEF: 'British Rail apologizes for the late running of this train and **for any inconvenience that it may have caused.'** This is all right as far as it goes but, to be on the safe side, it is best repeated about twelve times, very slowly, over a loudspeaker. You should be careful, however, not to give anything away regarding what has caused the delay. If trains arrive late it is **because of late departure** (never mind why that occurred). Similarly, at airports, planes are late in taking off **because of the late arrival of the incoming plane.** In fact, it is best not to go into this sort of detail at all. Things happen – or, rather, don't happen – **for operational reasons.**

All these expressions pale, however, beside that great British Rail number: 'This train is now approaching Runcorn. If you are leaving the train here, **please make sure you have all your luggage and belongings with you.'**

Shakespeare!

issue, bread and butter: not to be confused with 'beer and sandwiches at No.10', which are no longer obtainable.

light, in the ... of: usually 'recent experience'.

literally:

matter, the crux of the:
name it, you: } see **nutshell,** in a:
no way:

nutshell, in a: try 'In a nutshell, the crux of the mater is that no way are my members going to literally starve to death with regard to this one. I mean, you name it, we've rejected it ...'

ongoing: best combined with 'situation'. See below.

perspective, get it into:

point, can I just make this:

scenario:

situation: a NALGO operative (I assume), working for the Royal Borough of Windsor and Maidenhead, wrote to a householder in 1981 and asked him to a trim a hedge. He did so in these words: 'Whereas a hedge situation at Altwood Road, Maidenhead in Berkshire, belonging to you overhangs the highway known as Altwood Road, Maidenhead aforesaid, so as to endanger or obstruct the passage of pedestrians ...' That's the way!

Yoko Ono is quoted in *The Love you Make* (Peter Brown & Steven Gaines, Macmillan, 1983) as saying: '[John Lennon] asked if I had ever tried it [heroin]. I told him that while he was in India with the Maharishi, I had a sniff of it in a party situation.' Well done, Yoko!

table, at the negotiating:

time, at this moment (point) in: an excellent literary example from two stalwarts of the NUJ – 'The Marines, of course, had other ideas, but fortune was not favouring them at this moment in time.' (Robert McGowan and Jeremy Hands, *Don't Cry For Me, Sergeant Major*, Futura Books, 1983)

totally unacceptable: a useful phrase when you are just about to give in and accept such demands.

viable:

(Carried by a show of hands.)

In The Executive Washroom

Businessmen the world over should always seek to emulate their American counterparts and use the appropriate language – even if they are not entirely sure what a 'ballpark' is:

What Is A Ballpark?

Aspiring executives should practise saying the following phrases in front of the mirror in the executive washroom and see where it gets them:

'No **brownie points** in that for us, I'm afraid.'
'It does not **go on all fours**.'
'That's not in our **game plan**[1].'
'It's a **whole new ball-game**[2].'

Feel better for that? Absolutely essential in advertising circles, but also useful elsewhere, is the basic expression of an intention to try something out – **Let's/and** – which takes numerous forms:

'Let's run it up the flagpole and see if anyone salutes it.'
'Let's put it on the porch and see if the cat will eat it.'
'Let's put it on the train and see if it gets off at Westport.'
'Let's put it on the 5.15 and see if it gets off at Westchester.'

[1] Or, as used by R. Nixon, former used car dealer: 'We have to game plan this.'
[2] As used perfectly by G. Fernback, chairman of ABTA's retail travel agents' council: 'For the first time British Airways is making the right noises. It's a whole new ball-game now ... it's in their interest and ours that cheap tickets are available to the public.' (*The Times*, 26 September 1983)

'Let's leave it in the water overnight and see if it springs any leaks.'
'Let me just pull something out of the hat here and see if it hops for us.'

Having mastered these basic phrases with a **one foot in the water approach**, the business person should proceed to speak entirely in clichés – **it won't cost an arm and a leg**. He just has to **bite the bullet** even if he is **between a rock and a hard place**. Just let those ideas **bubble up**, proceed to **knife and fork** a solution, and prevent the whole **ball of wax** from becoming a **can of worms**.

Then he will be able to **get down to the nitty-gritty** and stop any **rattlesnakes from crawling out of the woodwork**. When he has most of the **players in place**, the opposition's **snow-job** won't have a **snowball in hell's chance** of **coming at him from left field**.

If he thinks all this is a bit **iffy**, he had better **orchestrate a scenario** of his own. But, frankly, I think it has the makings of a **womb-to-tomb deal**.

What To Tell Your Secretary To Say
Girl Fridays should learn to say: **he is not available today** or **he is not by his phone**. This could mean anything.

An Incidental Word of Advice
It is best not to have it off with your secretary at the office. Wait until you get home.

Books Do Furnish A Cliché

'Of making many books there is no end.' You can say that again, Ecclesiastes! Books do indeed pour out of every orifice – except, of course, the one that happens to be out of stock and is the one you want. Still, never mind. Publishing, bookselling and authoring keep quite a few mad people safely whingeing away at each other when they might otherwise be at your throat. Should you happen to stumble into this world, here are some useful hints to have up your sleeve:

The Naming Of Books

All books should be called **The Joy of** something. The first people to have this excellent idea were American cookery experts I.S. Rombauer and M.R. Becker. They called their book of recipes *The Joy of Cooking*. Then along came A. Comfort with *The Joy of Sex* which was so successful he soon came again with *More Joy of Sex*. Then everyone joined in. On my shelves I see such interesting tomes as:

The Joy of Computers
The Joy of Chicken (sic)
The Joy of Cheesecake
The Joy of Breastfeeding
The Joy of Geraniums, to name but a few.

Rather second best, but still quite good, are books given the title **Everything You Always Wanted To Know About ... But Were Afraid To Ask**. D. Reuben MD was the first to do this with his book on sex. Then came:

Everything That Linguists Have Always Wanted To

> *Know About Logic But Were Ashamed To Ask*
> *Everything You Always Wanted To Know About Drinking Problems And Then A Few Things You Didn't Want To Know*
> *Everything You Always Wanted To Know About Elementary Statistics But Were Afraid To Ask*
> *Everything You Always Wanted To Know About Mergers, Acquisitions And Divestitures But Didn't Know Whom To Ask*
> *Everything You Wanted To Know About Sports But Didn't Know Where To Ask*
> *Everything You Wanted To Know About The Catholic Church But Were Too Pious To Ask*
> *Everything You Wanted To Know About The Catholic Church But Were Too Weak To Ask*, and many, many more.

We had thought of calling this book *Everything You Always Wanted To Know About Clichés But Never Got Around To Asking*. Alas, someone else had got there first.

Equally entertaining are titles incorporating the following:

> **Confessions of a …**
> **The Complete …**
> **The Compleat …**
> **The Essential …**
> **Great … of the World**
> **The World of …**
> **The Wit and Wisdom of …**
> **How Long Will … Survive**
> **Anatomy of a …**
> **The … Factor**
> **The … Connection**
> **The … File**
> **The Good … Guide** (as in Food,
Hotel, Book, Pub, Museums, Software, Sex, etc. etc.)

The Writing of the Biographical Note

An excellent example of the potted biog. can be found at the beginning or on the jacket of this book. Copy it out for use concerning the author of any book except a) detective fiction (where frequently no biographical details are given, in a bid to heighten the air of mystery, and b) romantic fiction.

With romantic fiction it is chiefly important that the biographical details should describe a *woman*, even if, in fact, the author is a retired Colonel in the Argyll and Sutherland Highlanders. Perhaps the best I can do is to quote from the excellent jacket of *Dangerous Engagement* by Caroline Courtney (published by Arlington Books in 1980):

> 'Caroline Courtney was born in India, the youngest daughter of a British Army Colonel stationed there in the troubled years after the First World War. Her first husband, a Royal Air Force pilot, was tragically killed in the closing stages of the Second World War. She later remarried and now lives with her second husband, a retired barrister, in a beautiful 17th century house in Cornwall. They have three children, two sons and a daughter, all of whom are now married, and four grandchildren …
>
> 'She enjoys gardening and listening to music … she is also an avid reader of romantic poetry …
>
> 'Caroline Courtney … has written an enormous number of novels over the years – purely for pleasure – and has never before been interested in seeing them reach publication. However, at her family's insistence she has now relented …'

But what about her pets? you may ask. Unfortunately, I am unable to reproduce here the charming portrait of Caroline Courtney in which she is quite plainly nursing a friendly pug.

Incidentally, in case any of my remarks are misconstrued, I should make it plain that Mrs Courtney is *not* a retired Colonel from the Argyll and Sutherland Highlanders.

The Writing Of The Blurb

A few notes are necessary to supplement the descriptive blurb on this book's cover, which is only fair of its kind.

Firstly, you have got to describe the book which the reader wishes to buy, even if this may not have a great deal to do with the book you have written. Hence Tolstoy's *War and Peace* is:

> like its subject, a phenomenon
> a first-rate yarn,
> contains raw excitement,
> and tells the truth behind something,
> – not to mention provoking a laugh-a-page!

First Novelists write:

> a brilliant, inventive and often hilarious account
> or a devastating satire,
> incorporate dazzling and funny characterizations,
> and are hailed as the most exciting new voice to be heard in fiction since the war
> when they are not writing in the tradition of someone else.

Biographies, on the other hand:

> take the lid off things
> with razor-sharp accuracy
> amount to the definitive portrait,
> and are always about possibly the most controversial and charismatic personality of the century (note the 'possibly').

Autobiographies result in:

> a warm, nostalgic and revealing portrait,
> tell a heart-warming rags-to-riches story,
> and offer an intimate glimpse,
> a fascinating glimpse,
> a tell-tale glimpse,
> of perhaps the best-loved whoever it is.

Thrillers invariably present their heroes:

> caught up in a sinister maze (or web) of plot and double-cross.

Coffee-table books are:

a **verbal and visual feast**.

Humorous books offer:
>   **tongue-in-cheek impressions,**
>   **a chortle on every page,**
>   are **wickedly funny,**
>   and **deliciously capture the flavour of the radio series**.

They are best summed up as '**Hilarious! (Evening News)'**

Whatever the book, without question, **it is a social document of our time**. Above all, try and find a reviewer who is willing to be quoted as saying: **I implore you to read this book**. That shouldn't be too difficult.

Remember, when promoting a book, that it is only fair to the author to describe it as the best thing ever to have hit the bookshops. The author expects this and is likely to get very stroppy if you try and get him to settle for anything less. Hence, you should use such expressions as:

>   **another bestseller**
>   (no one is quite sure what a bestseller is – least of all people who compile bestseller lists – so it is quite in order to use this term even before the book goes on sale.)
>   **No. 1 bestseller**
>   (should only be used selectively – as everyone else will be using it.)
>   **for all seasons**
>   (as in, '*The Country Diary of an Edwardian Lady* is a book for all seasons'. So, for that matter, is *The Sex Maniac's Diary*.)
>   **from the author of**
>   (as in, 'Another bestseller from the author of *Watership Down, The Lord of the Rings, The Previous Better Book*, etc.')
>   **A modern classic**
>   (you're reading one.)

Put all these elements together and you get the sort of thing devised to promote a romantic novel. I spotted it in *The Bookseller*:

>   'The latest bestseller from Anne Mather ...

'Anne Mather is the world-renowned writer of romance. She has written over 90 novels and each has sold almost a million copies worldwide. 'Last year, Worldwide[1] published Anne Mather's *Stormspell*. It was a huge, runaway success. Now, in the same triumphant tradition, comes *Wild Concerto*. It is a searing story of love and heartbreak, revenge and soaring passion, set in the glamorous world of a top concert pianist and a girl who once loved him from afar.'

Wow!

My own personal favourite is the line which informs the potential reader that the book 'makes so-and-so look like a so-and-so'. When the *Daily Telegraph* reviewed Alan Sillitoe's novel *Saturday Night and Sunday Morning* in 1958 it called it a 'novel of today with a freshness and raw fury that makes *Room at the Top* look like a vicarage tea-party.'

When Jacqueline Susann's *Valley of the Dolls* came out, a publication called *This Week* noted that it made '*Peyton Place* look like a Bobbsey Twins escapade'. I'm not totally sure what a Bobbsey Twins escapade is but I'm pretty sure the criticism put Grace Metalious in her place.

On that score, THE JOY OF CLICHÉS makes *The Joy of Sex* look like *Zen and the Art of Motorcycle Maintenance*.

(I'm still working on this one.)

Writing The Book

This is a relatively simple and straightforward matter in comparison with promoting it. You just have to nail yourself to a seat and write. However, T. Morgan in his definitive biography of S. Maugham, writer and confirmed divorcé, (Jonathan Cape, 1980) lists one or two useful phrases as used by the master craftsman himself. His characters:

[1] (Ah, that's what they mean by 'sold worldwide'!)

get along **like a house on fire**
don't care a **row of pins** for each other
exchange **sardonic grins** and **disparaging glances**
are as clever as a **bagful of monkeys**
have beauty which **takes your breath away**
have a friend who is a **damned good sort**
meet a villain who is an **unmitigated scoundrel**
encounter a bore who **talks your head off**
have hearts which beat **nineteen to the dozen**
see the **unimaginable beauty** of far-away places.

For all of which he should surely have been given a Somerset Maugham Award.

Further guidance may be obtained from the work of S. Conran, ace novelist and Superperson. She is very strong on situations and on placing action at a specific time and place so that her readers can identify with the characters. In *Lace* (Simon & Schuster, 1982) after one character has had an abortion she orders a hot drink:

'She sat and sipped it, feeling the sun and the warm steam on her face **as a jukebox pumped out the new Beatles hit, "She Loves You".**'

S. Conran has also come up with another original idea — that the male orgasm resembles something else. If you can't think of anything else yourself, you should just follow Shirley's excellent example:

'Maxine was now heedless of anything except her urgent need for Charles, and their sexual tension swiftly built up to a climax **as violently explosive as the cork bursting from a bottle of champagne.**'

And, again, Shirley has a very good metaphor for one of her heroes:

'He captivated women with his fierce, proud face, his lean, well-exercised body, and his aura of sexuality, **wild as that of a stallion.**'

As you can see, this is all very straightforward and you will soon get the hang of it.

Writing Romantic Novels

These require even more subtlety and I am most grateful to Mrs C. Courtney, wizard of the genre, for much of the following guidance.

It might seem, to the uninitiated, that there is only one plot viz. **boy meets girl** and that all the romantic fiction writer has to do is prevent them falling into each other's arms or going up the aisle too soon. But this is to ignore the ever-increasing specialization of this type of novel, e.g:

> *Sensuous Romance* (also known as *Hot Historicals* or *Bodice Rippers* – boy meets girl but they actually Make Love before marriage);
>
> *Blue Rinse Romance* (boy meets girl but they only kiss);
>
> *Religious Romance* (boy meets girl meets God);
>
> *Medical Romance* (doctor meets nurse);
>
> *Teenage Romance* (boy meets girl meets Maths test);
>
> *Second Time Around Romance* (divorced man meets divorcée);
>
> *Granny Romance* (the heroine is over thirty);
>
> *Gay Romance* (boy meets boy) and *Ethnic Romance* (black boy meets black girl) have been experimented with in the US but not found to be commercial;
>
> *Terminal Romance* (boy meets girl meets death) has so far only been rumoured – though Erich Segal's *Love Story* was clearly headed in the right direction.

Despite these specializations, the reader of romantic novels basically requires the same elements every time she sits down to read one. These elements are:

1 The Hero

The one invariable rule is that, by the end of the book, the **hero must be extremely rich**.

His face is also very important and usually in some way **hard**. (It is a sign of Blue Rinse Romance that the hardness is emphasized. Indeed, in a Blue Rinse romance it is the only thing *allowed* to be hard.) For example:

> 'The intervening years since she'd last seen him had hardened his male features into implacable lines. The curve of his cheekbone was harsh; his jaw unyielding.'

(Janet Dailey, *Terms of Surrender*, Silhouette Special Edition, 1982)

His fingers should usually be long and sensitive:

'He placed his hands on the desk, fine-fingered hands that looked as strong as steel.'

(Kathryn Blair, *Children's Nurse*, Mills & Boon, 1981)

(There is, of course, more permissible hardness here for the Blue Rinsers.)

In these Doctor-Nurse Romances, fingers – sensitive and strong – often play a medical part in opening episodes:

' "Let me take over while you give mouth to mouth resuscitation." Strong hands slid into place on the man's chest as Sara obeyed without protest.'

(Sonia Deane, *Bachelor Doctor*, Mills & Boon, 1982)

The hero's gaze is almost always **hard**, too. Positively steely:

'The brim of his hat shadowed his eyes, giving him a hooded look. Angie caught their glitter, but it wasn't the silver brilliance that used to excite her. When he took a step forward, she saw that they held the glitter of polished steel, sharp and cutting.'

(*Terms of Surrender*)

(At this point, the prudent heroine lowers her eyes before the steely-cold provocation.)

Alternatively, when not steely, **the hero's eyes rove** either **lazily or slowly:**

'His all-seeing gaze sliding down her soft, rounded, almost naked body in slow appraisal.'

(Patricia Lake, *Wipe Away the Tears*, Mills & Boon, 1982)

'Steadily he gazed at her face as if lazily deciding whether he would take further sport at her expense.'

(Caroline Courtney, *Libertine in Love*, Columbine House, 1982)

Nowadays, romances are allowed to hint at **other things** about the hero, as well as faces and gazes, that **are hard**. This is known as 'putting in a bit of steam'. However, anatomical vagueness remains the order of the day:

'He was very tanned, strong and physically fit, his skin like oiled teak over powerful muscles and sinews. Brief black swimming trunks revealed [not what you might think but] his hard flat stomach and strong thighs.'

(*Wipe Away the Tears*)

It is especially effective, of course, if you can combine the hero's hands (roaming) with the necessary hardness:

'All the while his hands roamed over her body, manipulating and exciting Angie to a point of frenzy. She strained toward him, seeking the gratification his hard manhood promised.'

(*Terms of Surrender*)

Another way of achieving this effect is by use of the key word 'virility':

'His fingers teased until her nipples hardened to desire, and in a great upsurge of longing, she arched her body to the coiled-spring inflexibility of his. Little moans of ecstasy escaped her as she strove to come even closer to the taut muscles of his loins ... the glow of lips moist from his kisses seemed to drive him to madness and she was crushed again into the punishing strength of his arms, the male hardness of his virility stimulating every nerve fibre in her body until there was only the chaos of burning need of fulfilment, a need that was a wild unabridged desire for the feel of his naked flesh against hers ...'

(Anne Hampson, *Stormy Masquerade*, Silhouette, 1980)

(Thank you, Anne.)

While I remember: nasty pieces of work (male) who are finally brought to heel must admit: **you have taught me the true meaning of the word 'love' for the first time.**

2 The Heroine

The chief thing to remember about heroines is that they are capable of an enormous range of sensation from very little physical contact. **A mere touch of the hand is enough to get them going:**

> 'Max Bellmer took her hand in his and drew it to his hard mouth, brushing her palm briefly with his warm lips. Jassy quivered, his touch tingling fire that shot through her whole body.'

(All this before we get to the first kiss:)

> 'Suddenly she was in his arms ... His lips touched hers, gently as the flutter of a butterfly's wing. Her breath almost stopped at that first magic contact.
>
> 'Then his mouth came down on her harder and closer and more demanding. She could see his eyes blazing with passion, as he drew her close to him. She could feel the buttons of his black coat pressing into her.
>
> 'She knew she ought to struggle against his embrace ... that this was wrong ... but she could not. Her breath was coming in quick pants, while she could feel him breathing as if he had been running ... with a little, half muffled cry, she returned the kiss and melted into his strong arms.'

(*Wipe Away the Tears*)

You should also remember that the romantic heroine has **a tendency to bury her head in the hero's jacket.** This, one might say, is the kiss diverted:

> 'With a jerk she was pulled against him and his arms were about her so tightly that she could hardly breathe, her face pressed into the thick soft material of his jacket front.'

(Anne Neville, *Gold in Her Hair*, Circle of Love, 1982)

'With a little cry, Juliana flung herself against him, burying her face in his waistcoat.'

(Caroline Courtney, *Libertine in Love*, Columbine House, 1982)

3 The Barbara Cartland Heroine

All B. Cartland's **heroines are virgins**. They can readily be identified by their **heart-shaped faces**:

'In all the long years of his life he had never seen anything quite so exquisite as her fair hair which at times seemed almost to have a touch of fire in it and framed her heart-shaped face.'

(*The Judgement of Love*, Arrow Books, 1980)

The other mark of a Cartland heroine is a **complexion** variously **described in horticultural terms**:

'Never before could he remember seeing hair that appeared almost like a shaft of sunshine against the dark panelling of the hall, and her complexion was as pink-and-white as the almond blossom on the trees outside.'

(*The Twists and Turns of Love*, Arrow Books, 1978)

The other major peculiarity of a Cartland heroine, and to a lesser extent the hero too, is a plethora of **dots** in speech. They all seem to pause a lot, probably to convey a fabulously breathless emotion. Here is a post-coital bedroom conversation. The happy couple are married, it must be pointed out. (The moment at which the virginity was lost was tastefully described this way: 'Then in the silence there was a soft, sweet cry, but it was not one of fear.') Here goes:

' "I did not frighten you?" he asked.

' "You know that ... everything was ... unbelievably wonderful ... I did not think that ... love could be ... so perfect, so good and yet so ... exciting."

' "I want to ... excite you."

' "You made me feel … as if I touched … the stars … and yet I was … wild … like the wind."
' "That is what I want to make you feel, my precious little love."
'She quivered because he was caressing her, then she whispered:
' "I want to … ask you … something."
' "What is it, my darling?"
' "Do you … think that … you have … given me a baby?" '
(*The Wild, Unwilling Wife*, Pan Books, 1977)

4 The Asterisk

Asterisks, which have disappeared from most books, still survive in romance. Lovemaking itself dissolves into asterisks in Blue Rinse Romance:

'Up the long staircase, below the glittering chandeliers, the Duke carried his bride …

* * *

'Later, much later, he looked down upon the slim body that was now lying beside his own.'
(Caroline Courtney, *Duchess in Disguise*, Arlington Books, 1979)

5 The Clothes

Clothes are a very important accessory in historical novels. They are particularly stressed in Regency romance. The Regency hero always has **skin tight pantaloons** and **glossy boots**:

'Miss Massingham reminded herself that this elegant gentleman, with his great shoulders setting off a coat of blue superfine, and his shapely leg encased in a skin-tight pantaloon and a Hessian boot of dazzling gloss, was the bouncing baby on whom thirty years before, she had bestowed a coral rattle.'
(Georgette Heyer, *Pistols for Two*, Pan

Books, 1976)

Also, in Regency romances the villain, if there is one, can usually be recognized by his **addiction to jewellery**.

6 The Ultimate Plot Explanation

This occurs in the last chapter, either just before the final kiss or just after. It usually contains **explanations for delay or quite unreasonable behaviour** by both the hero and the heroine. In historical novels, these can be quite elaborate:

> 'Then as she nestled contentedly against him, he resumed his story. "I think I was like one crazed or drugged. I just went scrabbling up the broken wall and across roofs where tiles lay shattered, many of them loose … The elephants were charging down the main thoroughfare leading to the western gate so my aim, if I had one at all, was to work my way to one of the numerous side alleys".'
>
> (Rose Hughes, *The Dangerous Goddess*, Mills & Boon, 1982)

This explanation goes on for several paragraphs culminating in the moment when Adam finishes his tale. It is now time for the heroine's:

> 'As if reading her thoughts, Adam said gently, "Can you tell me what happened in the ruins of Amber? Everything, my darling?"'

She can and does. Another example:

> ' "I know all that," said the Earl, and for the first time he smiled directly at her. "When I saw you leave the ballroom, I could not be sure why you had left, and when I saw Sir Samuel's coach disappearing, then I admit I thought it must be an elopement. Directly he took the Dover road, I knew that even if you had joined him willingly, you must have been deceived into thinking he was going to Gretna Green …" '

These writing hints for romantic novels can easily be applied to other kinds of fiction. For example, The Ultimate

Plot Explanation is equally a must for detective stories. It is all a matter of common sense really. But I look forward to reading the fruits of your pen.

*   *   *1

Writing For Radio

All the above guidance can be applied to writing short stories and plays for radio. The only other thing to remember is to include as many **sound-effects** (seagulls, footsteps, clocks chiming) as possible and **have your characters continually explain what they are doing** ('Oh, I'm just about to go through the door, darling ... ah, that's better'.) Whenever your characters put on articles of clothing they should go 'Aaaah!', as if they are having a bit of a struggle.

When writing scripts for *The Archers* – or for soap-operas in general – you should incorporate two expressions as often as you possibly can. N. Painting, actor, writer and part-time Bruno Milna, advises the inclusion of:

why are you telling me all this? (followed by a long and detailed explanation)

and: **I see what you mean.**

See what I mean?

---

1 (No, this does not signify love-making, merely a change of subject.)

Unaccustomed As I Am

Whether you are proposing the health of bride and groom at a wedding or responding on behalf of guests at a rugby club dinner — or perhaps both — there are plenty of things you can say to help you cope with what is to most people rather an ordeal (i.e. listening to your speech).

It is essential to start by saying **unaccustomed as I am to public speaking** ... There is a very good precedent for this. When W. Churchill, valiant war leader and bricklayer, made his first ever public speech at Bath in July 1897, he said:

> 'If it were pardonable in any speaker to begin with the well worn and time honoured apology, "unaccustomed as I am to public speaking," it would be pardonable in my case, for the honour I am enjoying at the moment of addressing an audience of my fellow countrymen and women is the first honour of the kind I have ever received.' (*Cheers*)

This seems unnecessarily cautious on the great man's part but, happily, it did not affect his subsequent illustrious speaking career. If it was good enough for him, it is good enough for you. Bung it in.

N. Coward, entertainer and tax-exile, was wont to begin his speeches with the words, 'Terribly accustomed as I am to public speaking.' This should not be attempted by beginners, however.

Once you have got this first sentence out of the way, it is downhill from then on. Remember, many people get called upon to make a speech, but it always seems to be you who is chosen. So keep it short and stick to this useful skeleton formula:

A Useful Speech For Every Occasion

'Your Majesty/
Your Royal Highness/
My Lord Mayor/
Mr Chairman/
Headmaster/
Friends of the Bride/
Fellow Odd-Fellows/
Gentlemen of the Press/
Ladies of the Night/
and Members of the Institute of Concrete Technology ...

   'On this auspicious occasion, it gives me great
pleasure to propose a toast on behalf of:
my fellow bridesmaids/
the Old Sodomites First XV/
the boys of the school/
my very lovely lady wife ...

   'It reminds me of:
the story of the Admiral and the Bishop/
the Bishop and the actress/
the actress and the parking meter/
of when I was sitting where you are now/
of an incident in Virginia's childhood ...

   'I should like to put in a special word for:
those of you who haven't won any prizes
today/
Mrs Maggs who did the flower
arrangements/
Virginia and Michael – who are just about
to go upstairs and put their things
together ...

   'And so, in conclusion, I would ask you to
join me:
in having much pleasure/
in asking for a well-deserved half-holiday/
in declaring open this fête worse than death/
in thanking your glasses/

in raising the bridesmaids/
in responding on behalf of the toast.
'Thank you very much …'

That should see you through all right.

Dear Sir Or Madam

Many people find writing letters a terrible chore. It is a fact, however, that a lot of the difficulty can be taken out of correspondence by the judicious use of cliché. Rub just a few clichés together and, in no time, you will find a letter forming before your eyes. You will hardly realize you are writing it.

Writing To A Disc Jockey

Let me give you an example. You want to write the simplest of notes to a radio DJ asking him to play a request for someone you know.

Step one is to take a postcard (because it is **postcards only, please**).

Step two: write 'Dear ———'. Do not put the DJ's name in the space. Put **favourite DJ**.

Step three: write 'Please play ———'. Do not put the title of a record. Put **any record**.

Step four: write 'For ———'. Do not put the name of any old relative. Put **for the best Mum in the world**.

Step five: Do not put that it is her birthday. Put **she is 97 years young**.

Step six: Put **tell her we are all missing her very much** (even if you're not).

Step seven: Put 'Love, Tracey X X X'

If you do not hear your request being played after making use of this simple formula, your postcard must have got lost in the post.

Writing To A Newspaper

Having mastered this simple technique, it is now possible to apply it to other areas. For example, there may be some

burning issue you want to write to the papers about.
Whatever it is, this is the form:

'Dear Sir,

'My attention has been drawn to the recent comments
in your newspaper concerning ... ...

> (this suggests that either you are much too
> busy to read the papers yourself and have a
> highly-paid operative who scans them for
> you, or, that you don't usually dirty your
> hands by reading *this* piece of chip shop
> fodder. That is certainly the view of CAC
> member, the Rt Revd David Cyril-Lord, who
> pioneered the technique.)

'Speaking as the father of two teenage daughters ...
(very important this.)

'I didn't fight through two World Wars in order to see
this happening in our country ...

> (like the previous line, this sentiment will also
> earn you a round of applause should you
> ever get a chance to utter them on radio's
> *Any Questions.)*

> 'I remain, Sir, yours faithfully ...'
> (when writing to *The Times* you may disguise
> your lack of faith by using the form 'Yours
> &c', whatever that may mean.)

Writing Holiday Postcards

Over one hundred years of postcard writing
have not seen any significant improvement
on the basic message: **having a wonderful
time – wish you were here**. A pity, however,
that so many people neglect to put an 'x'
somewhere on the other side of the card with
the note 'This is our hotel' or 'This is our
room' – even on pictures of the Sahara desert
or the Great Australian Bight.

Writing Business Letters

It is courteous to end business letters with either:

1 **Thank you in anticipation**

or:

2 **Thank you for your time and consideration**

or both.

It is a stylish idea to have your notepaper headed:

From the desk of (followed by your name).

Alas, this allows clever-dicks of the N. Coward variety to write back with letters beginning 'Dear Desk ...' Never mind.

A nice warm touch is to sign off with:

Dictated by Mr —— and signed in his absence.

Writing Business Replies

Only two expressions may be used and not usually in the same letter:

1 **We must arrange to have lunch some day.**

2 **Our cheque is in the post.**

Writing Bread-And-Butter Letters (1)

When you have been to stay with people for the weekend, the form is as follows:

'Dear ...

'Thank you for such a lovely weekend.

'**It was a real treat for us to get out of London into the country**/into London out of the country ...

'**... such a lovely part of the country**/ atmospheric corner of London, too ...

'**It was a wonderful rest from our usual weekend chores** ...

'The Point-to-Point/ your dog **was great fun** ...

'**The roads were surprisingly clear on the**

way back ... we were back in London/
in the country in under an hour ...
    'Thank you again ...'

Writing Bread-And-Butter Letters (2)

On receiving gifts – especially wedding presents – there is, again, a very simple formula for thanking the giver:
    'Dear ...
    'Thank you ever so much for the lovely ——
    'Though we have eleven toast racks and three laundry baskets, until your —— arrived, we hadn't been given a single ——.
    'It looks lovely against the grey walls of our sitting room and cheers us up whenever we look at it ...
    'It will always remind us of you and the happy times we spent at ——'
    'Thank you again for the ——.'

Writing Bread-And-Butter Letters (3)

Children find thank-you letters even harder to write than adults. They should go in for the utmost brevity. The following is an actual letter I received from a small male relative and should serve as a model:
    'Dear ...
    'Thank you very much for your card and three pound postal order. I am not sure what I am going to spend it on yet. I might get some more sweets or another book. But whatever I spend it on it will be very useful. On Wednesday part of the playing field was under water.
    'I hope you are well,
    'Love ...'

Writing Kiss-Off Letters

I was once sitting in a tea-house near St Albans when I overheard a most extraordinary conversation taking place. It was about a man who was always chucking out his live-in girl friends – so much so that he had established a rate for the job. If they went without tears or fuss they were rewarded with a mink and a Mini.

I realized there and then that kissing-off was a subject I knew nothing about. I still don't, and so I consulted CAC member Christopher Ferrat who is always doing it. He recommends the following:

1 Begin with: **Some letters are as hard to write as they are to receive. This is one such ...**

2 **I've been thinking about our relationship ...**

3 **I wonder if you agree with me that when you can't grow, go?**

4 End with: **I hope we will always be friends.**

(To get the right effect – Christopher says – you should tear up the letter and burst into tears several times before sending it.)

Writing Fan Letters

It is a very embarrassing matter to express your admiration for the talents of/stand taken by/physical charms of a public figure, in a letter. Wishing, as always, to be of assistance I have constructed an all-purpose fan letter which will serve to enchant the actor/author/politician/broadcaster/bit of crumpet of your choice. Here goes:

'**Dear Terry:**

> (always plunge in on Christian name terms. After all the subject of a fan's attentions is public property. However, you may like to add – **I hope you don't mind me calling you that, but I feel as if I already know you.** Best not to use this method when writing to Sir John Gielgud. Try putting 'Gorgeous Conk' instead.)

> '**I always enjoy watching you on the telly**/hearing you on the radio/reading your books/seeing your films ...

> '**I think you/it/they are the best thing on TV**/radio/in the cinema/the House of Commons/my local library ...

> '**One needs a good laugh in these difficult**

times, as I always say ...

(this is bound to go down well when writing to such fun people as T. Benn, N. Tebbit, S. Rushdie, P. Anne.)

'**Please believe an ordinary housewife** when she tells you ...

'**Keep up the good work**/we are right behind you here in Chislehurst/can I fondle your tits?

'**Any chance of a photograph?**

'**PS I always have to be prepared with several hankies** to catch my tears of laughter when you're on ...

'**PPS I enclose an SAE for your reply ...**'

Incidentally, it is a nice touch if Radio 4 listeners add at the bottom of their letters: **Please excuse writing. Eyesight failing**.

While we are on the subject of approaching celebrities, I should perhaps mention that if you ever encounter one in the flesh what you are supposed to say is: **Oh, it's Mr Bernard Levin, isn't it?** or **Is this *the* Mr Bernard Levin?** This gives the celebrity the chance of replying wittily, 'No, but I used to be' or 'No, I'm the other one.'

If it is not Bernard Levin, this form of inquiry will probably elicit who it really is.

When asking for an autograph, it is usual to add: **It's not for me, it's for my daughter**.

Wish You Were Here

Travel Brochures

For the average holidaymaker, a trip to the seaside or overseas is a time for relaxation. He should not have to concern himself with clichés beyond the obligatory **having a wonderful time** and **wish you were here** on his postcard home (see previous section). It is more important to leave such matters for the tour operators and travel agents to worry about.

Even in this department, help is at hand. When describing the delights of travel there are certain colourful phrases which can be applied to any resort in any country. When compiling next year's brochures, travel agents should use the following description, inserting the appropriate place names – be they Benidorm, Port Said or Lowestoft – in the spaces provided:

The 21-day World Highlights tour to (e.g. LOWES-TOFT) is a **once in a lifetime experience**.

In its 307,374 square miles —— **offers a variety of scenery which is second to none.**

Set in a **storybook land of spectacular, natural and man-made wonders,** —— is an **island paradise** that is **saturated with serenity. It is an island haven of peace and tranquillity.**

Here you will find:
    sun, sand and sea/
    sunkissed beaches/
    waving palms/
    miles of golden sand/
    sparkling turquoise seas/
    palm-fringed beaches

and **beaches that are fringed with palm trees.**
In the 21 action-packed days you will experience:
the thrill of a lifetime,/
an **unforgettable holiday experience,**/
and **all that you have ever dreamed about.**

LOWESTOFT is to be found in a setting not far from a country of **burning deserts – said to be the world's largest –** which act as a **silent witness** to countless invasions from **time immemorial.**
Regrettably they are gone now, but **they have left behind their romantic atmosphere** in their **ancient jewel of a city** with its **maze of narrow alleys.**
Majestic, snow-clad peaks with their **tree-clad slopes** crowded with **majestic pines,** beside **crystal clear lakes,** act as a **Mecca for people of all nationalities** who wish to follow **in the steps of** Marco Polo.
The hills beckon the rambler on countless lovely walks in the **time-honoured tradition of old.**
Romantic —— is the ideal destination for the discerning traveller intent on **getting away from it all.**
Its **quality hotels** are renowned for their **award-winning cuisine,** offering **good food** and **fine wines** in a **tastefully-furnished** setting of **traditional chalet-style comfort.**
Just **relax in one of ——'s cafés, sipping a cool drink, nestling peacefully beside** the main railway station.
Time has passed by this **quiet bywater, full of Nordic charm.**
—— is a **place to which you will want to return year after year.**
And so **we must reluctantly say farewell** to **——**.
(I could go on like this for ever, you know.)

Our Reporter
Made A Cliché And Left

It may have been Arthur Christiansen, one of the numerous former editors of the *Daily Express*, who once posted a sign in the office saying: 'ALL CLICHÉS SHOULD BE AVOIDED LIKE THE PLAGUE.' The message is clear: people may tell you to, but there is no avoiding the cliché. So journalists should simply lie back and employ it.

Phrases That No Self-Respecting Journalist
Could Possibly Manage Without

Although basically intended for the printed page these phrases can also sound very attractive when spoken by radio and television journalists.

I am indebted to the many fine journalists (and fellow members of the NUJ, let's not forget) whose notable contributions are appended as examples to be followed.

Remember, scribes, it is not sufficient to get only one or two clichés in per piece. You should blend them together. Really stuff 'em in!

Please study the list carefully. At the end of it you will be tested on the knowledge you have acquired:

alarm bells ringing, this news has already set: example – 'The trio moved off in a yellow Mini and as they drove west the resemblance between Mr Waldorf and Martin began to ring alarm bells among the police.' (Stewart Tendler, *The Times*, 20 October 1983)

alive and well and living in: it is never enough to say that some faded star of yesteryear is still alive (e.g. in answer to the question **Where are they now?**) The faded star is 'alive and well and living in Godalming'. And who the hell *was* Jacques Brel in the first place?

amid mounting: *only* journalists are allowed to use this phrase. It has nothing to do with horses or sex but is a useful way of linking two otherwise unrelated subjects, e.g.: 'Amid mounting calls for his resignation, Mr Nixon held a pre-arranged pow-wow with the Girl Scouts of America.'

– and that's official: instead of 'according to a report just published by the Institute of Concrete Technology, we will all be dead shortly', it is so much more appealing if you say: 'We'll all be dead shortly – and that's official.'

anguish → joy: in all cases, 'A young mother's anguish turns to joy'. Or *vice versa*.

as we know it: when part of our heritage is threatened, it is a good ploy to emphasize that we know or knew it. Thus, 'England losing the World Cup would mean an end to civilization as we know it.'

at five minutes past eight on the evening of 23 July …: absolutely mandatory *Sunday Times* style. It gives you more insight.

at the end of the day: not to be confused with the previous entry. Usually best reserved for conversation, though occasional written use can be allowed: 'Many of the participants feel that at the end of the day, the effects of the affair [the abortion debate in the Irish Republic] will stretch far beyond the mere question of the amendment.' (Patrick Bishop, *The Observer*, 4 September 1983) (See also MY CLICHÉ AND I and ONGOING INDUSTRIAL ACTION).

award-winning: we all know this is meaningless, but it makes a useful variation on 'distinguished' (see IN A PACKED PROGRAMME TONIGHT).

blow the whistle on: 'English as she is murdered on radio became an issue once more. Alvar Lidell stamped his foot and blew the whistle in *The Listener*.' (Anne Karpf, *The Listener*, 3 January 1980)

BRIDES: without exception, a woman on her wedding day, however ugly or closely related to the Queen, is described as a **radiant bride**. If she is, or has ever been, remotely keen on swimming, she is described as **taking the plunge**.

cash your chips: greying TV reporter T. Mangold wrote in *The Listener* (8 September 1983) concerning the US arms race in space: 'Under malign command, a technological guarantee of invulnerability could induce the holder to cash his chips and go for a pre-emptive first strike.' That, presumably, is also **when the chips are down**. Thank you Acting Wing Commander V. Noble for drawing this to my attention.

charisma: only politicians and **captains of industry** tend to have one of these, whatever it is. But you'll recognize it if you ever see one with it.

company director: in court reports, this means either 'crook' or 'just anybody'. I know, I am one.

confirmed bachelor: as far as I can tell, this is the best way of describing people like E. Heath, Prime Minister and helmsman. After all, he is not married and is a communicant member of the Church of England. He also plays the organ by himself and collects bone china.

constant companions: like water, these run hot and cold. See 'model' and 'fun-loving', which the terms is **not unrelated to**.

could make any ordinary girl feel like a princess: in February 1983, the Press Council reported on the curious case of Miss Carol Ann Jones and the *News of the World*. Miss Jones had been quoted by a N.O.W. journalist as having opined that Peter Sutcliffe, the Yorkshire Ripper, 'could make any ordinary girl from a mill town feel like a princess. Even now I have a place in my heart for him.'

The Press Council felt that 'some words and phrases attributed to her as direct quotations were ones she was unlikely to have used.'

Clearly what the Bingley girl really said was that the Yorkshire Ripper **could make you feel like Cinderella before the clock struck.**

I am not prepared to comment on the connection between these phrases and the celebrated dictum regarding W. Simpson, noted divorcée and D. of Windsor: 'She could make a matchstick seem like a Havana cigar.'

COURTS: bad-hats are always tried in **the historic No. 1 court at the Old Bailey.** Frankly, my dear, if it's not historic, it's not the No.1 court at the Old Bailey.

DASHES: you can never use enough of these. How about: 'MOTHER-OF-FIVE IN GET-ME-TO-THE-CHURCH-ON-TIME DRAMA'?

dream → nightmare: e.g. 'Mrs Craddock's dream holiday turned into a nightmare when her husband was eaten by the Loch Ness Monster.' Dreams may also be found in the company of cottages, and nightmares in conjunction with alleys.

drive another nail in the coffin: a pleasing image, best enhanced with an unusual adjective or two – as in, 'This British soccer bluesday drove another nail into the tottering coffin of Britain's Barons of Ball and Caliphs of Kick.' (I am most grateful to D. Frost, tele-host and v.w. person, for this example.)

exclusive: the most important word in any journalist's lexicon. For example, when a visiting film star gives a press conference at the Savoy, the twenty-four journalists who attend will each label his 'interview' 'exclusive'. There is nothing contradictory about this. Each journalist is merely reporting the version of the interview he himself heard with his own two ears. What he writes is his exclusive version of the proceedings.

Even when an individual reporter or newspaper is genuinely first with a story, other newspapers will pick it up from the first edition and reprint it. So, at most, the exclusivity will last perhaps an hour. Do not be discouraged. It is still an exclusive and you must use the format: **I can exclusively reveal that** ...

extraordinaire: it gives a taste of the exotic and Continental when you write that someone is a '—— extraordinaire!' – '[Culture Club's] flexible eight-piece includes Steve Grainger's sax, Terry Bailey's trumpet, Phil Pickett's keyboards, and their secret weapon, Helen Terry, a backing singer extraordinaire.' (Max Bell, *The Times*, 27 September 1983)

Not to be confused with *oo-la-la*! which refers to something else. However, 'French lovely Zizi Blancmange is an oo-la-la girl extraordinaire!' would be quite acceptable.

FASHION: there are several rules to be observed when describing the Spring and Autumn Collections, i.e. **the Fashion Stakes**.

1) **Spring is** always **in the hair**
2) **Necklines** always **take the plunge**
3) **You can't go wrong with a thong**, though more likely you'll be **going for a thong**.

(I am most grateful to S. Menkes, Fashion Editor of *The Times*, for pointing these out to me.)

flight from fear: this must always be used literally and involve actual aeroplanes. E.g.:

> 'TO BRITAIN ON FLIGHT FROM FEAR
> 'A flight from fear ended at Heathrow Airport yesterday for passengers on the first plane to arrive from Poland since martial law was proclaimed at the weekend.' (Jon Ryan, *Daily Mail*, 18 December 1981)

Where possible the flight number should be given.

FUNERALS: descriptions of burials need a lot of 'they' i.e. mourners, relatives of the dead, whole communities etc.:

'They came, 541 of them, across half a world to dedicate the war memorial on a treeless hillside above Blue Beach, where British forces first stepped ashore.' (Alan Hamilton, San Carlos Sound, *The Times*, 11 April 1983)

Also useful: **They buried their own** ... and **the flower of their** ...

fun-loving: it has been suggested that this epithet may hint at rather more than what it says – as in, 'Fun-loving top-model Nikki Norris, 22, from West Paddington, likes cuddling her poodle under lamp-posts.' Maybe. See also under 'constant companion' and 'model'.

—— **gate**: in the wake of Watergate – the name, lest it be forgot, of an apartment block in Washington DC – it has become standard practice to apply the suffix '—— gate' to any political scandal: Koreagate, Lancegate, Billygate, Liffeygate, and so on. Debategate and Briefingate were applied to the flap in 1983 over how Ronald Reagan's campaign team got hold of President Carter's briefing books before a 1980 campaign debate on TV.

The useful thing about the '—— gate' suffix is that it immediately indicates that a scandal has occurred and doesn't just suggest the possibility.

guilty men: once upon a time, M. Foot, politician and dog-walker, collaborated with other journalists in writing a best-selling pamphlet called 'Guilty Men'. This was in July 1940 and described N. Chamberlain, politician and paper-waver, and others who had led us into the Second World War.

The term can now be applied to anybody, even if not guilty, using the phrase: **We name the guilty men**.

hard-pressed: British manufacturing industry always is.

HEADLINES: the following is a simple but infallible guide to headline-writing. Select three words at random, one from each of the lists below, and – bingo! – you have a headline. What could be simpler?

AXE	LOOMS	SHOCK
BAN	MONSTER	STALKS
BID	MOVE	STORM
CALL	PLEA	STRIKE
CLAMPDOWN	PROBE	SURVIVOR
DASH	RIDDLE	TERROR
FEAR	ROW	TEST
HORROR	SEX-ROMP	THREAT
LEAK		

If you still can't get the hang of it, how about:
>SEX-ROMP STRIKE LOOMS

or   AXED BAN BID

or   CLAMPDOWN DASH ROW?

(Well, *I* know what they mean.)

helping the police with their inquiries: no, don't laugh at this! The fact that some poor innocent is alternately being beaten senseless and offered cigarettes by the boys in blue is nothing unusual. He is genuinely helping police with their inquiries. They would like to know whether he is a murderer/rapist/bad egg and he is helping them find out, in spite of any appearances to the contrary.

in-depth: means superficial but proud of it.

in the heart of ———: when you wish to say that something is in the middle of somewhere, it adds a nice touch if you say it is 'in the heart of London's theatre-land' or 'in the heart of Parkinson country'.

in the pipeline: as in, 'Sheikh Yamani said a new round of OPEC talks was in the pipeline' (well, he would, wouldn't he?)

intrepid: reserved for any aviatrix or lady yachtsperson e.g. S. Scott or C. Francis.

journey into the unknown: although any journey is potentially this, a good example occurred at the start of the

Falklands business: 'To the strains of "We are Sailing" the ropes were slipped and *Canberra* was off into the unknown.' (Jeremy Hands and Robert McGowan, *Don't Cry for Me, Sergeant-Major*, Futura Books 1983)

let the last word be with: see 'word, last'.

living a lie: 'Zany Kenny Everett's wife kept her love affair secret from the outside world for 4 years – to save hurting his feelings. Cuddly Ken knew of the affair. But Lee Everett and her lover, Sweeney actor John Atkin, lived a lie to avoid publicity.' (*News of the World*, 2 October 1983)

PS Disc jockey and somewhat unstable fun-person, K. Everett, told me in an exclusive interview that he *hates* being described as 'zany'. Pay no attention to the little fellow.

London's ——: it may seem a bit odd to write 'I was walking down London's Oxford Street' or 'I was visiting London's Tower of London' but it is vital to identifying the wider context. After all, there is an Oxford Street in Manchester. For all we know, there may be a Tower of London there, too.

Extend the use with other clichés – always 'London's fashionable Belgravia' or 'London's historic Tower of London'. Every little bit helps.

long, hot summer: oh, William Hardcastle, where are you now? They really had long, hot summers in the 1960s. They were hot because black chaps set fire to cities like Detroit. They were long because W. Hardcastle used to go on and on about them in his popular radio programme *The World at One*. But a spark survives: 'It looks as if it will be a long hot summer for the dons of Christ's College, Cambridge, who are once again faced with the tricky business of electing a Master.' (Lady Olga Maitland, *Sunday Express*, 11 July 1982)

looking bronzed and fit: film stars and such like people always manage to step off planes, following a **well-earned rest**, looking this way, rather than crumpled and irate like the rest of us. No, don't ask me how they do it.

major: not a rank in the army, but the invariable accompaniment to such delights as setback, reason, outbreak, in-depth probe, etc. 'Knock, knock' – 'Who's there?' – 'Major' – 'Major who?' – 'Major Setback!'

Man, the …: as in 'The … Man' (Magic Man, Music Man, Graffiti Man, etc.): 'Barry Manilow, the Music Man, flew into London yesterday. It is hoped to have it rebuilt by the Spring.' A variation on the following –

Mr ——: any supremo should automatically be dubbed 'Mr ——'. *Private Eye* showed the way with 'Soccer's Mr Football'. Michael Baily, for example, followed in *The Times* (8 December 1981) with: 'London's new Mr Railway, David Kirby, likes messing about in boats and singing in the choir …'

model: many a subtle distinction here. A girl who is a mere 'model' does not do a great deal of modelling, though she might like to. So she has to bend over backwards to participate in other activities. A **top model** may have modelled once but she is now too busy having affairs with pop singers and being photographed without the clothes she used to model. An **ex-model** means she's having to do some 'modelling' on the side.

See also 'constant companion' and 'fun-loving'.

moment of truth: you do not have to be a bull-fighter about to stick it in to say 'This is the moment of truth' ('El momento de la verdad'). Try it whenever your back is up against it – if you'll pardon the expression.

must surely kiss goodbye: as in, 'Spurs, unless they extract their digit, must surely kiss goodbye to their fans and any hopes of world soccer supremacy.'

mystery girl/mystery man: useful when you haven't a clue who it is you're writing about.

name of the game: as in, 'I think one has to say that

Monopoly is the name of the game'.

Nazi jackboots: when describing the run-up to the Second World War, the sound of the Nazi jackboot is much in evidence. Suggestion: 'The Nazi jackboots were singing their swansong'. It's worth a try.

never be the same again: any change, however unremarkable, requires this phrase. For example: 'When Mary Martin first opened her mouth in *South Pacific* in London's historic Drury Lane Theatre, one thing was clear: the Broadway musical would never be the same again.' Use as often as possible, occasionally substituting **marked the beginning of a new era.**

nude: in journalism, people are never 'naked', always nude.

—— **of the century:** the use of this handy verbal gadget in the title of a TV quiz hosted by Nicholas Parsons – *Sale of the Century* – should encourage you to use it more often. It is most useful and distinctive when naming things about which it would otherwise be rather hard to say anything good.

Savour this use of the phrase in an ad for *Time* in 1983 (beneath a photo of the Prince and Princess of Wales):
> 'Theirs is a **storybook romance.**
> 'The wedding of the century, a royal birth, the magic and splendor that surround a future king and queen have **captured the imagination of people everywhere** ...'

on the road to nowhere: not to be confused with 'journey into the unknown'.

one small step for ——, **one giant leap for** ——: handcrafted, this one, by N. Armstrong, astronaut and quotable person. Insert the words of your choice in the comfort of your own home. E.g. 'SMALL STEP FOR NON-WHITE MANKIND' (*The Times*, 29 October 1983)

one step forward, two steps back: not to be confused with the above. N. Lenin, rail-traveller and comrade, once wrote a book with this title – full marks! How interesting that R. Grant, astrologer and larger-than-life fat person, should still be writing in the *Chiswick and Brent Gazette* (22 September 1983):

> 'GEMINI (May 22/June 21) It's been a one-step-forward-two-steps-backwards time.'

Alternatively, use 'two steps forward, one step back'.

our reporter made an excuse and left: because, having encouraged vice-girl Roxy to confess all, she offered to make him a cup of tea. It is possible that she did, in fact, go further and that she **committed an act which we cannot describe in a family newspaper.** Whether our reporter joined in or departed before, during or after this atrocious behaviour is unfortunately impossible to say, at this stage. His expenses were not unusually high that week. Give him the benefit of the doubt. Only proper.

parameters: no, we're not sure what they are either, but it is good to have them by you in case you ever need them.

perhaps: caution is always a good thing: it saves you having to deal with idiot readers who write to disagree with your assumptions. 'To mark the magazine's 60th anniversary, *Time* this week is bringing out a separate, special issue that recalls the years since 1923, perhaps the most astonishing six decades in history.' (John A. Meyers, *Time*, 10 October 1983)

The same applies in broadcasting. Encouraged by the attitude of my superiors, I once attempted – alas, unsuccessfully – to persuade J. de Manio, broadcaster and horologist, to begin the *Today* programme by saying: 'Good morning, perhaps.'

POLITICS: when reporting leaks from Government ministers and Whitehall officials, the following phrases are mandatory and a must:

> **sources close to the Prime Minister say**
> = the Prime Minister told me ...

in Prime Ministerial circles it is being said that
= everyone including the milkman is saying that ...

it is being suggested in Whitehall that
= while passing the Cenotaph in a taxi it occurred to me that
or I went and stood there and made this up ...

a reliable source has stated that
= a source who has not let me down *so far* has said ...

I can now reveal that
= I've just about got enough evidence to go on ...

an official spokesman said today
= I had to take this from the bloody press handout.

recipe for disaster: lots of things are this – and not just when a Fleet Street journalist is anticipating a busy day **when the jumbo-jet crashes in the Strand** or the **Boeing lands on Buckingham Palace.**

redraw the map: this is always accomplished singlehandedly – quite an achievement – as in, 'Shirley Williams has singlehandedly redrawn the political map of Britain.'

rest is history: useful when you have run out of space or time and have to finish quickly what you are writing, as in: 'There across all the papers was the photograph of me presenting the Queen Mother with her chart, under the caption "Astrologer Royal". Well, the rest as they say, is history.' (Russell Grant, *TV Times*, 15 October 1983)

ring of steel: a real beauty, this, for when the heavy stuff gets rolled out in a war-situation. Full marks to *The Times* (30 April 1982) for this headline use, and explanation:
  'RING OF STEEL AROUND ISLANDS
  'The 200-mile total exclusion zone around the Falkland Islands, within which all unauthorized ships and aircraft run the risk of being attacked,

comes into operation at noon (British Summer Time) today. The most demanding responsibility, that of keeping out Argentine aircraft, will fall upon the 20 Sea Harriers with the Royal Navy task force, and the three type-42 destroyers with their Sea Dart anti-aircraft missiles.'

Runner-up: 'SYRIAN STEEL RINGS ARAFAT' (*Sunday Express*, 8 October 1983)

Also ran: 'The place [Warsaw] is just a ring of steel.' (Mike Davis, BBC TV *Nine O'Clock News*, 17 December 1981)

riddle: when no one can make head nor tail of something it is not a mystery, a problem or a conundrum. It is unquestionably a riddle e.g.: 'RIDDLE OF MONSTER FISH IN LAKELAND RIVER' (*Sunday Express*, 18 September 1983)

rules OK: as in 'Golf Rules OK?' (*Observer* headline, 13 November 1983)

self-appointed: tin-pot dictators are.

self-styled: tin-pot dictators are, when they call themselves 'emperor'.

shame: 'THE SHAME OF OUR PRISONS' was the headline over an editorial in *The Observer* (3 May 1981). For variety, you may also apply this formula to hospitals, cities and schools. Not to be confused with those sexual activities which may only be accomplished with difficulty in prisons, hospitals and schools, for which you subsequently express regret viz. **our night of shame**.

shockwaves: are much felt – 'When the Biba empire finally toppled, the shock waves were felt so far abroad that it seemed unbelievable that they were caused by what was really only a smallish shop in a smallish city.' (Sally Brompton, *Observer*, 4 September 1983)

so-called: as in, 'The so-called "dream ticket" of Mr Neil Kinnock and Mr Roy Hattersley was safely in the clasp of the Labour Party leadership last night' (Ian Aitken, *Guardian*, 3 October 1983 – page 1) and, 'The trade unions emphatically endorsed the so-called dream ticket coupling of Mr Neil Kinnock and Mr Roy Hattersley for the leadership and the deputy leadership of the Labour Party' (Keith Harper, *Guardian*, 3 October 1983 – page 24.)

spelled love: 'The Ding-Ding special that spelled love for Sid and Jan Parker will take a trip down memory lane ... to celebrate their 25th wedding anniversary. The happy couple will kiss and cuddle on the top deck of the No.44 bus, just like they did when they were courting.' (Janet Midwinter, *Sun*, 15 October 1983)

SPORT: see chapter entitled WINNING IS WHAT IT'S ALL ABOUT.

stalks: not what connects vegetables and plants to the earth but what fear invariably does to the streets e.g.:
AIDS FEAR STALKS THE CITY OF TERROR
(or alternatively)
AIDS TERROR STALKS THE CITY OF FEAR

star/starring: some confusion has arisen over the correct use of the word 'star' in relation to actors who appear in films and plays and to other people who take part in radio and TV programmes. These guidelines should help:
1) anybody who is appearing in stage, film, radio or TV productions should be described as a 'star' and 'starring in'. Carrying a spear at Stratford? Got a walk-on part in *Crossroads*? Doing the boring old weather forecast? You are a star, dear.
2) the word 'actor' should only be applied to film, theatre and TV 'appearers' who are very distinguished or who are unemployed.
3) if people do not qualify as stars under this definition they

are quite obviously 'audience', 'viewers' or 'bums on seats' and should be described as such.

tell it like it is: people should. This is in no way dated Sixties talk. No way.

that almost got away: by analogy to big fish – as in, 'The Bond film that almost got away.'

that says it all: in picture captions, this invariably applies to a 'look' or 'smile'.

that was once: an essential piece of survival kit for the intrepid war correspondent: 'As I stand here in the blazing ruin that was once Beirut/Belfast/the largest supermarket in Brixton, bullets whistle past me ...'

they call/called/are calling: whoever 'they' may be – and one trusts they are people to whom the journalist has actually talked and been properly introduced – they certainly do a lot of calling. Note: If 'they' are calling 'it' the 'street of shame', they are probably fellow journalists and should be avoided. Equally useful in TV news, this one, and especially successful when combined with other clichés. In 1981, at the nuptials of Prince Charles and Lady Diana Spencer, They Were Calling It The Wedding Of The Century, quite rightly. Some more examples:

> '... in what they are calling the South African Aberfan.'
>
> (Martyn Lewis, ITN's *The Making of '81*)
>
> 'Alfredo Astiz drank free champagne in seat 9A of the executive suite on a British Caledonian DC10 flight to Rio yesterday. The man they call Captain Death was being returned to his homeland via Brazil.'
>
> (John Passmore, *Daily Mail*, 12 June 1982)
>
> 'They called it paradise. Now burnt-out cars litter the roads, some the tombs of drivers who could not beat the flames.'
>
> (Brian Timms of Reuters, Melbourne, *The*

Times, 19 February 1983)

(the) thinking person's ——: as long ago as 1931, Pebeco toothpaste (in the US) was being promoted as 'The Toothpaste For Thinking People'. Quite who was qualified to use Pebeco and what they had to think about while they used it, is unfortunately not known to me. However, I think it was F. Muir, wit and bow-tie supporter, who set the more recent trend going when he talked of 'the thinking person's crumpet – Joan Bakewell.' Then along came droll people who talked of 'the thinking person's Rodin' (who could they mean?), and this fine selection:

> 'Frank Delaney – the thinking man's Russell Harty' (*The Sunday Times*, 16 October 1983)
> 'Frank Delaney – the thinking man's Terry Wogan' (*Guardian*, 17 October 1983)
> 'the thinking woman's Terry Wogan, TV's Frank Delaney' (*Sunday Express*, 30 October 1983).

TRANSPORT: some of the most vivid clichés are derived from transport e.g.:
> **on the rails**
> **off the track**
> **going full steam ahead**

Needless to say, these are best not used in a transport context-situation.

unacceptable face of ——: for example, 'Edward Heath, the unacceptable face of confirmed bachelordom.'

wall, writing on the: graffiti, as in, 'Nigel Rees was a serious author and broadcaster until he saw the writing on the wall.' (D. Batey, ITV's *Look Who's Talking*, 30 November 1983)

WEATHER: take care with **phew, what a scorcher!** as some people will unaccountably laugh at you. However, you are on safe ground with the following rules:
> 1) **temperatures** either **soar** or **plunge**
> 2) **Britain** always **swelters** or **shivers**

3) when snow and ice engulf us, weathermen invariably warn:
there's more to come, say weathermen
4) and when sun and heat smother us, weathermen invariably say:
but make the most of it, say weathermen.

wheel of fortune, the: has always 'come full circle for ...'

where are you now?: (with 'now that your country needs you' understood) e.g. Guy Fawkes, Jack the Ripper, Lord Lucan. Not to be confused with **where are they now?** – digging up people who were once news-worthy (a useful way of filling up pages on a thin day).

who made him what he is today: not a question – a mere statement of fact.

wild horses wouldn't drag it out of me: referring to her own list of recommendations as a judge of the Booker Prize, L. Purves, brief editrix of *Tatler* magazine, warned: 'Wild horses would not make me tell you anything more about it.' (*Listener*, September 1983)

will the real —— please stand up!: especially useful in headlines e.g. 'WILL THE REAL TOULOUSE-LAUT-REC PLEASE STAND UP!'

winter of discontent: first of all, congratulations to W. Shakespeare, playwright of Stratford-upon-Avon, for his very inventive opening of *The Tragedy of King Richard III*:
'Now is the winter of our discontent
Made glorious summer by this sun of York.'
Next, felicitations to numerous British politicians c.1978-9 who sensitively used this phrase to describe the **industrial action** (i.e. inaction) during the winter of 1978-9.
It could be argued that the clever use of this quotation helped bring down the government of J. Callaghan and made way for the triumph of M. Thatcher. But this was a joint effort by the politicos and the lads of Fleet Street.
A special award to *The Observer* (7 February 1982) for

extending the use into a new field with the headline: 'WHY FOOTBALL MUST SURVIVE ITS WINTER OF PENURY AND DISCONTENT'.

Even Shakespeare would have been pleased with that.

with —— like that, who needs ——?: originally, 'friends' and 'enemies', though the variations are innumerable: e.g. tits/coconuts.

word, last: see 'Let the last word be with'.

A Note To The Public

Do not be alarmed should you ever become newsworthy yourself and/or get interviewed by the gentlemen of the press. They are very helpful people and will gladly put words in your mouth if you can't think what to say. However, if you memorize the following list and repeat it, this will save the reporters a great deal of bother.

These phrases may also be used when submitting letters to newspapers for possible publication – indeed, they will help ensure that your contribution is included.

Thank you.

When puzzled about absolutely anything, you should exclaim:

why-oh-why?

You should always describe yourself as:

a mere housewife

When embarrassed about anything (and hoping to win £5 for your letter) always say:

was my face red?!

When you stumble upon a burglar's horde/pop star's closet, report that:

it was like an Aladdin's cave in there

After a fire, an explosion or teenage party, recall:

it was worse than the blitz

> (compare: 'Mr David Steele ... in a Volkswagen van which was behind the Mini carrying Mr Waldorf [was asked about the number of police officers he saw]: "I saw one, then two, then it

was World War Two all over again".' (*Daily Telegraph*, 14 October 1983)

After a teenage party, riot, football supporters' trip abroad, assert:

they were like animals

All behaviour, accommodation, compensation payment, is:

not good enough

All young people:

drive like maniacs

All dead spectators, road accident victims, ordinary folk who get hurt:

never had a chance

When asked about the lover with whom you have just been holed up for forty-eight hours:

we are just good friends (it could be true!)

When wishing to appear sophisticated, whatever the occasion, say:

no comment

> (note the clever variant introduced by D. Wilcox, TV executive and husband, in 1980: 'Sorry, your camera's run out of film.' And remember what happened to Martha 'The Mouth' Mitchell, Watergate wife and telephone girl, who said: 'I don't believe in that "No comment" business. I always have a comment.')

When wishing to express joy, say that you are:

over the moon

> (it is a mistake to restrict this phrase to sport. When M. Albert Roux, chef, won three Michelin stars for his Mayfair restaurant, 'Le Gavroche', he told *The Times* (21 January 1982): 'I am over the moon.')

When wishing to express sadness, say that you are:

sick as a parrot

When describing what happened as you came out of your hotel bedroom, say:

we saw this ball of fire coming towards us

When a miracle happens, it is always:
like a dream come true
> (prize-winning examples: 'British radio hams are
> to be able to talk to an astronaut on board the
> latest US space shuttle ... Dr Garriott said:
> "This will be a dream come true. I have had this
> project on my mind since I first became an
> astronaut." ' (*The Times*, October 1983) 'A club
> cricket enthusiast has inherited a fortune and his
> own village cricket club from an elderly widow
> who was a distant relative he never knew ... Mr
> Hews, aged 68, a retired company representa-
> tive, lives in a semi-detached house in Arnold
> Avenue, Coventry. "It's like a dream come
> true," he said.' (*The Times*, 22 October 1983)

It is of great help if you can supply the reporter (and thus
his readers) with as much useful, incidental information as
you can. E.g. after a fire rescue:
> 'I snatched up my daughter, **aged 3**, and my
> son, **aged 2**, and ran for safety.'

After a ferry fire:
> 'I ordered: "Stop the **electrically-controlled**
> capstan".'

Please also note that when having your picture taken you
should – whatever the circumstances:
a) **show a bit of leg** (if you are female)
b) **give a thumbs up sign** (if male, even if
covered from head to toe in bandages)
c) **carry your bride over the threshold**.

If you do not do any of these things and simply smile
moronically at the camera, the caption-writer will be forced
to put that you are **seen enjoying a joke**.

Thank you again.

Test Paper

Find out how much you have learned or consolidated by
reading the above chapter. Imagine you are a reporter or
sub-editor on a newspaper. Firstly, complete the following

word-pairs to round off the sentence, e.g. 'the helicopter pilot went on a MERCY-*DASH*'. Not all the word-pairs have been mentioned in the chapter so far. The answers are at the end. The Editor's decision is final.

1) the helicopter pilot went on a MERCY-
2) the judge handed down a SAVAGE-
3) Cyril Smith is a CONFIRMED-
4) the pop-star arrived with his CONSTANT-
5) Jean Harlow was the first BLONDE-
6) brothers, we are involved in an ONGOING-
7) he departed from Heathrow with a blonde MYSTERY-
8) the professor sat surrounded by DUSTY-
9) 'Will the ratings stay up if Roland Rat departs, that will be the ACID-
10) police rushed to cope with the latest BOMB-
11) the Home Secretary is having to consider DRACONIAN-
12) there has to be a way out of our current INDUSTRIAL-
13) Mike Kevin files this ON-THE-SPOT-
14) 'I love diamonds and champagne too much,' quipped the MERRY-
15) police immediately launched a NATIONWIDE-
16) the Government does not wish to inaugurate another PAY-
17) the winners set off straightaway on a SPENDING-
18) the St John's Ambulance men were the UNSUNG-
19) Oxford undergraduates today took part in an IRREVERENT-
20) 'I do not believe the views put forward by these SO-CALLED-

Now, complete the following sentences with the appropriate word or phrase:

21) the bride was –
22) around this war-torn city is –
23) in the – No 1 court at the Old Bailey
24) he was faced with a sea of –
25) the shame of our –

26) they indulged in a night of —
27) they set off on a flight from —
28) 'We are over the —
29) after this, one thing is certain —
30) she fought back the —
31) the rest is —
32) they set off on a voyage into the —
33) we have been living a —
34) Mike Kevin is reporting from far-flung —
35) woolly-minded —
36) the finger of —
37) tug-of —
38) their faces showed all the emotion of —
39) 'I am disgusted. There is no —
40) he elevated it to —
41) the village that —
42) the ship that —
43) the feathers really —
44) without question, the dormitory had become a sin —
45) the Minister has slapped a —
46) — struck when ...
47) a pall of fear —
48) is there a mother in the land whose —
49) the dollar took a —
50) battle lines are —
51) the disgraced Minister was last night maintaining —
52) I plan to give my baby away, says —
53) it could only be described as a hidden cesspit of —
54) innocent women and —
55) before a — court-room
56) she was involved in — goings-on.
57) the Soviets were involved in naked —
58) early in her career she took part in — movies
59) 'All right, it's a fair —,' said the driver
60) 'I'm very upset about his death because he taught me —

Lastly, what do the following nicknames, epithets or euphemisms actually mean or refer to?

61) angels
62) larger-than life

63) Billy Bunter
64) shapely
65) attractive
66) svelte
67) dashing
68) stunning
69) tempestuous
70) vivacious
71) quietly-spoken / well-mannered / fastidiously dressed
72) bachelor girl
73) bachelor
74) former convent girl
75) an old-fashioned girl at heart

Answers To Test Paper

1) dash
2) indictment
3) bachelor
4) companion
5) bombshell
6) situation
7) girl
8) tomes
9) test
10) outrage
11) measures
12) action / malaise
13) report
14) widow
15) hunt / search
16) freeze /bonanza
17) spree
18) heroes
19) spoof
20) experts
21) radiant
22) a ring of steel
23) historic

24) upturned faces
25) prisons / hospitals / schools
26) shame / passion
27) fear
28) moon
29) things will never be the same again
30) tears
31) history
32) unknown
33) lie
34) trouble spots
35) liberals
36) suspicion
37) love
38) a slab of granite
39) other word for it
40) art
41) died
42) died of shame
43) flew
44) bin
45) ban on
46) tragedy
47) hangs heavy over the strife-torn city today
48) heart does not go out in sympathy?
49) pounding
50) being drawn up
51) a dignified silence
52) mother-to-be
53) vice and degradation
54) children
55) packed / hushed
56) naughty
57) aggression
58) sizzling
59) cop
60) all I know
61) nurses

62) fat
63) fat
64) sexy, with big tits
65) sexy, with small tits
66) sexy, with no tits at all
67) fancies himself
68) sexy, but a nut-cracker
69) gets drunk in restaurants
70) noisy / a bit too much of a personality girl (and vice versa)
71) poof
72) raver with own flat
73) poof / eccentric
74) right little raver
75) takes after her mother

Score Analysis

Award yourself one point for a correct answer. Out of a possible 75, if you have scored:

Between 0 and 20: you are of a sensitive disposition, probably a confirmed bachelor, and should very seriously consider whether it will do your health any good to continue reading this book.

21-40: you are Bernard Levin and would do well to start using shorter sentences before you get any older.

41-60: it is not too late for you to enroll at one of the CAC's Summer Schools. I feel that the bracing air of Milton Keynes coupled with a course of lectures from such luminaries as David Vine, Alan Whicker and Prof. Ernst Tlint might just about tip the balance in your favour.

61-70: a job awaits you working behind the scenes of BBC TV's *Breakfast Time*. You are clearly getting the hang of things and should be pleased that your investment in the cost of this book is bearing fruit.

70 and over: you are the editor of the *Sun* newspaper. You are finding it very difficult to read this book without moving your lips. But then, you have no need of it. Good luck in whatever field you to choose to move into when the time comes.

Desert Island Cartoons

If you were to be cast away on a desert island which four cartoon situations would you choose to take with you? A close look at countless thousands of cartoons has led the CAC to conclude that there are four basic cartoon situations. Cartoonists should not, therefore, bother to invent any new ones. These will suffice. All that it is necessary to do is invent new captions. But that is a minor job.

SITUATION 1

SITUATION 2

SITUATION 3

SITUATION 4

(There is, of course, another man underneath the bed.)

The Good Menu Guide

I can only think of one wine or food that is a cliché in itself – and that is **champagne**. This is because it is inevitable. You have something to celebrate – you have a ship to launch, you want to do something disgusting with an actress's slipper – so you pop open a bottle of champagne! You would not think of celebrating with dandelion and burdock, would you? You wouldn't launch a ship with Grand Marnier. You wouldn't drink brandy out of an actress's slipper any more than you would accept mouth-to-mouth resuscitation from a St Bernard. The answer is always champagne. If you are into flaunting your homosexuality, you drink nothing else anyway.

All this means, however, that to find clichés elsewhere in the world of oral gratification you have to look not in the pantry or the drinks cupboard but at the menu:

A Candle-Lit Supper

Almost invariably you will find that the **menu is in French**. This is only sensible as it adds an air of mystery and excitement to eating out. How much more interesting to order 'pamplemousse', not knowing what it is, than to find out straightaway that it is boring old grapefruit?

A menu written in English can still tempt and delight, even so. It helps, of course, if the restaurant has a name like **'Michael's'** and is advertised as providing **country fare in traditional English style** or **English fare served in a friendly atmosphere**. If the restaurant is to be found deep **in the heart of** Constable **country**, or some such area, and has a candle-lit dining room, so much the better. As long as **Good**

Things are to be had **for your delight**, that is all that matters.

If there is **morning-fresh** asparagus, followed by fish **blended with delicate spices** and **served in a special sauce**, followed by lamb that has **grazed on the heights of the sierra** and been **cooked by an age-old method**, you are probably in for a feast.

The *Good Food Guide* will probably conclude that the restaurant **displays flair** – though you can never be sure.

A Modest Little Wine-List

Wine-experts have a language all of their own and are probably best avoided. However, if they say the wine **has a good nose** or is a **modest little vintage** with or without a **sharp** or **burnished** edge and a **good body pushing about underneath**, you could well be all right. Avoid them if they say things like **makes your tongue resemble the bottom of a parrot's cage**.

A Word From The Proprietor

Is everything all right, sir?

Twelve Reasons Why ...

... You Should Use Clichés In Your Advertising Copy
The first thing to realize about advertising copy.
> Is that it should **be jerky.**
>> And **use short sentences and paragraphs.**
>>> For no apparent.
>>> Reason.
> Even if the paragraphs end up.
>> Having only one word in them.
>>> That will.
>>>> Do.
You'll soon get the idea.
> I don't who why it is.
>> I think it might have something to do.
>>> With copywriters' early.
>>>> Potty.
>>>>> Training.

The second thing to realize is that there are always:
TWELVE REASONS WHY YOU SHOULD BUY ANYTHING
1) It's a **new improved offer.**
2) It's the **best that money can buy.**
3) It contains a **new wonder device/miracle ingredient.**
4) It gives **added value.**
5) It is **revolutionary and NEW.**
6) It's the **Big One.**
7) There's **2p Off.**
8) It enables you to ask the question **Whatever happened to ...?**[1]

[1] e.g. 'Whatever Happened to Romance?' Coty perfume.

9) It is **country-fresh** and **like mother used to make.**

10) This is what advertising **is all about**[2].

11) **Every home should have one.**

12) **Happiness is** a worn cliché[3].

Twelve More Great Things To Say In Your Ads

1) **You, too ...** – as in, 'You, too, can have a body like mine.'

2) **Yes, Gluppo!** – the Affirmative Repetitive, as in:

BUTCH MALE V/O: Why not try Gluppo?
HOUSEWIFE: Gluppo?
BUTCH MALE V/O: *Yes,* Gluppo!

3) **Yours to enjoy in the privacy of your own home**

4) —— **now,** —— **later** – as in, 'Buy now, pay later', 'Go now, pay later', 'Sin now, repent later'.

5) **Mmmmmm, tasty!**

6) **Guaranteed!**

7) **Unique!** It's the ... **Experience!**

8) **Amazing!**

9) **Before/after**

10) **I love** (with a heart shape instead of the word 'love')

11) **Bonanza!**

12) **All** bargains are bargains 'which no housewife **can afford to ignore!'**

---

[2] 'Air France's Concorde. Rediscover what flying is all about.'
[3] 'Happiness is ... egg-shaped
    ... a quick-starting car
        ... a cigar called Hamlet
            ... being elected captain and getting a Bulova
                watch
                    ... a 49$ table
        ... a bathroom by Marion Wieder'

Another Quirky Twenty-Nine Phrases To Use With The Personal Approval of David Ogilvy:

1) **NEW**
2) **FREE**
3) **HOW TO**
4) **SUDDENLY**
5) **NOW**
6) **ANNOUNCING**
7) **INTRODUCING**
8) **IT'S HERE**
9) **JUST ARRIVED**
10) **IMPORTANT DEVELOPMENT**
11) **IMPROVEMENT**
12) **AMAZING**
13) **SENSATIONAL**
14) **REMARKABLE**
15) **REVOLUTIONARY**
16) **STARTLING**
17) **MIRACLE**
18) **MAGIC**
19) **OFFER**
20) **QUICK**
21) **EASY**
22) **WANTED**
23) **CHALLENGE**
24) **ADVICE TO**
25) **THE TRUTH ABOUT**
26) **COMPARE**
27) **BARGAIN**
28) **HURRY**
29) **LAST CHANCE**

D. Ogilvy, modest advertising guru, in his **seminal** *Confessions of an Advertising Man* (Athenaeum, 1962), adds: 'Don't turn up your nose at these clichés. They may be shopworn, but they work.'

Thank you, David, for providing us with a moment of much-needed uplift at this point in the book.

Winning Is What It's All About

Whether you are a sportsman or merely a commentator, there are some handy phrases which will help you describe the game you are involved with. Most of these phrases are transferable between the various popular sports – and, indeed, may be used in most areas of human life, but this is where they work with so much effect, **you can bank on it:**

Football

Players should not just score goals, they should:
stick the ball in the back of the net
When this occurs, then:
there'll be —— in the streets tonight
> (T. Stoppard, wordsmith and cliché connoisseur, suggests in his v. excellent play *Professional Foul*: 'There'll be Czechs bouncing in the streets of Prague tonight as bankruptcy stares English football in the face.'

Team managers should urge that:
the first 90 minutes are the most important
Sports journalists should advise their readers:
make no mistake
Players should comment on winning/losing by saying:
I'm over the moon/sick as a parrot[1]
And, more philosophically, state that:
winning – that's what soccer's all about.

[1] It is still correct form to use these phrases, in spite of Wally advice to the contrary.

Cricket

Fruity-voiced commentators should aver:
  that was a four from the moment it left the bat
Fruity-voiced commentators should sum up:
  throughout the match the pendulum swung to and fro
      (until it finally swung full circle.)

Tennis

When a player breaks a service, commentators should invariably say:
  now the thing to do is break straight back

All Sports

Everybody should say:
  winning is what it's all about
      (e.g. 'Whoever plays best is going to win ... this
      is what the game is all about' — Peter Purves,
      BBC TV *Championship Darts*, 22 September
      1983)
Journalists should write of tough characters:
  he makes Al Capone look like a choirboy
      (rarely found in ice-skating, however.)
At tense moments, commentators should always remark:
  you could hear a pin drop in here
      (if only the commentators would stop talking,
      you could.)
All sportsmen are best known by their nationalities rather than their names, viz.:
  the Englishman/the Spaniard
      (especially if they have peculiar names like
      Severiano Ballesteros.)
In defeat, they can but say:
  you can't win 'em all
      (this is also very useful in real life.)
In retrospect:
  it was going to be a long night.

The Movie They Said
Could Never Be Made

Hollywood, in recent years, despite S. Goldwyn's famous request, 'Let's have some new clichés', has been undergoing something of a crisis. Unwise pressure from critics and competition from other media has led to a reduction in the cliché-quotient of movie scripts. No wonder audiences have been dwindling!

In an effort to show the folly of this trend, I am printing here a rarely seen document taken from the MGM script archive. It is a treatment which is – to coin a phrase – the film script to end all film scripts. But its original purpose was to instruct writers new to Hollywood in certain technical matters. As such, it takes us back to Hollywood in **those golden days of yesteryear.** What a pity it is not known who compiled this dazzling compendium of clichés from the **Golden Age** of Hollywood! Of course, something is lost upon the printed page and the CAC has felt it necessary to update one or two elements in the treatment but I have high hopes that one day the film will grace the silver screen. Meanwhile, 'Lights!' 'Action!' – here it is:

GONE WITH THE CLICHÉ (Shooting script)

SCENE 1.   EXTERIOR.   A SMALL VILLAGE IN BAVARIA, 1812.   DAY.

(Caption: 'A small village in Bavaria, 1812'.   A four-wheeled

carriage passes by with its wheels going backwards.   Chickens

scuttle out of the way.)

SCENE 2.   INTERIOR.   THE CARRIAGE.   DAY.

(The Vicomte de Cliché (Tony Curtis) is seated with his intended

(Jack Lemmon))

THE VICOMTE (<u>taking out his watch</u>): How time flies! It is 1812 already. And **we're making a terrible mistake!**

HIS INTENDED: Napoleon has yet to be defeated at the Battle of Waterloo, i'faith! And **two can play at this game!**

THE VICOMTE: If only this coach would go faster...

HIS INTENDED: **One day,** perhaps, **they will invent some kind of iron horse that will** run on rails and carry us from Paris to Vienna in the twinkling of an eye.

THE VICOMTE: 'Twill never come to pass.

<u>(Pause)</u>
<u>(The Vicomte waves idly to a passer-by)</u>

HIS INTENDED: To whom are you waving, my lord?

THE VICOMTE: To that young whipper-snapper, van Beethoven. **Calls himself a composer. He'll never make it**, I'll be bound.

HIS INTENDED: Have you heard his music?

THE VICOMTE: He's as deaf as a post. He should stick to painting.

<u>SCENE 3. EXT. A FOREST IN A FILM STUDIO. NIGHT.</u>
<u>(The carriage passes through. Thunder and lightning. The</u>
<u>carriage overturns. The Vicomte and His Intended are thrown out</u>
<u>but unhurt.)</u>

THE VICOMTE: Follow me, I do believe there is a small forester's hut hereabouts. It is quite big, even if he is not. Perchance we can rest there until the storm has abated.

<u>SCENE 4. INT. THE SMALL FORESTER'S HUT. NIGHT.</u>
<u>(The Small Forester is bowing and scraping and acting rather a</u>
<u>lot.)</u>

SMALL FORESTER: You are welcome, sire.

THE VICOMTE: **Nice place you got here**[1]. - er, yes, thank you.

(The Small Forester exits.)

THE VICOMTE (<u>to His Intended</u>): **Get out of those wet clothes and put this blanket round you.**

HIS INTENDED: No, my Lord. **Would you be shocked if I put on something more comfortable?**

THE VICOMTE: As you wish.

(Pause. The Vicomte stirs the embers of the fire with a poker, but this time there are no faces to be seen in them. His Intended returns. She is clad only in bra, panties and glasses, but has her back to the camera. Cut to close up. She takes off her glasses and throws them over her shoulder.)

THE VICOMTE: **But, Miss Smith - you're beautiful!**

(His Intended kisses him passionately. They disappear out of the bottom of the frame in a clinch.)

SCENE 4A. INT. A CLINCH. NIGHT.

SCENE 5. EXT. MONTAGE. DAY.

(Passionate music. **Corn fields waving. Breakers on a sea-shore.**

[1] Noted connoisseurs, D. Vosburgh and T. Lyttleton, wrote a delightful song 'I Love A Film Cliché' which was included in the Broadway hit *A Day In Hollywood, A Night In The Ukraine.* In it they prefer the extended version of this phrase. It takes on a darker tone when uttered by a gent with lumps in his jacket. Viz. 'Nice place you got here, blue eyes. Be too bad if something was to … happen to it …'

This goes on for about two minutes. Caption: 'Came the Dawn...

SCENE 6. INT. THE SMALL FORESTER'S HUT. DAY.

(It is sunrise and light streams in through the window. The
couple lie languorously on a large bed. The Vicomte still has one
foot on the floor.)

HIS INTENDED: Must you go?

THE VICOMTE: **These are modern times!** Income tax is fourpence in
the pound. **A man's gotta do what a man's gotta do!**

HIS INTENDED: Yes, I know Geoff. **Your thing is bigger than both**
of us[2].

(She cries. Two young children - a boy and a girl - enter.)

MICKEY ROONEY (inevitably): Daddy, daddy, **why is mommy crying?**

THE VICOMTE: **She'll pull through, my boy. But she's gonna be a
mighty sick little lady for a while.**

JUDY GARLAND (for it is she, too): But mommy's leg is broken and
the curtain is due to go up in half-an-hour!!

THE VICOMTE: Son! Isn't there something you should have said to
me, 'ere now?

MICKEY ROONEY: Gee, sorry Pa! **Why don't we put on a show** --

JUDY GARLAND: -- **right here in the** Small Forester's Hut or **barn?**

THE VICOMTE: And you, daughter, will have to take the leading
part.

JUDY GARLAND: Gee, I'll try!

THE VICOMTE: **You'll be going out there a youngster, but you've**

[2] A colourful reading, this. More usually: 'This thing is bigger
than both of us.' Note the excellent use made of this type of
remark in the 1976 re-make of *King Kong*. Jeff Bridges says to
Jessica Lange: 'He's bigger than both of us, you know what I
mean?'

gotta come back a star![3]

JUDY GARLAND: !!

THE VICOMTE: There is no time to lose. You must learn this song.
(They go to the piano. After a hesitant start, **Judy Garland soon**
picks up the song, throws the music away and begins singing it
lustily with full orchestral accompaniment.)

SCENE 7. EXT. THE SKY. NIGHT.
(A Jumbo Jet is peacefully breasting the clouds. **Place names**
flash across the screen: 'SAN FRANCISCO...CHICAGO...NEW
YORK...PARIS...A SMALL FORESTER'S HUT...')

SCENE 8. INT. DR BIG'S CASTLE. NIGHT.
(Dr Big - Donald Pleasance, Orson Welles, o.n.o. - is immensely
evil. He has an artificial limb which is not immediately
apparent; he eats raw virgins for breakfast; and, of course, he
has a terrible foreign accent. Apart from this, he is not very
nice.)

DR BIG (looking through a telescope at the heavens): Ah ha! The
jet is on time. Soon I will have the world in my grasp. Ah ha!
That will compensate me for my terrible laugh and unspecified
artificial limb!
SIDE-KICK (his side-kick): But, Dr Big, **must you tamper with**
forces unknown?
DR BIG: My dear Side-Kick, there is no cause to be alarmed.
Can't you see that I am offering you eternal life?
SIDE-KICK: No.

[3] Many thanks to *42nd Street* (1933) for helping us out with
regard to this one. In that film, Ruby Keeler was the chorus-girl,
Warren Baxter played the producer, while Bebe Daniels had the
broken leg.

DR BIG: **You're just like all the others. You think I'm mad,**
don't you?

SIDE-KICK: Not mad, no, but how about <u>geisteskrank</u>?

DR BIG: Please! <u>Geisteskrank</u> **is such an <u>ugly</u> word!**

(<u>Ominous music mounts ominously</u>)

DR BIG: Pah! Side-Kick! **Those drums are driving me mad,** do you
hear?!

<u>SCENE 9. INT. BACKSTAGE AT THE SMALL FORESTER'S HUT. NIGHT.</u>
(<u>Judy Garland is having a triumph. Mickey Rooney has just</u>
<u>realised something - Judy Garland is a star and he is in lurv with</u>
<u>her.</u>)

MICKEY ROONEY: Gee, Judy, **you can't be that same freckle-faced**
kid with the braces on her teeth I used to know?

JUDY GARLAND: No, that's right, I'm not.

MICKEY ROONEY: Just a thought. Anyway, how about coming with me
and appearing in a sequel to this rubbish after the show?

JUDY GARLAND: Oh, no, I couldn't, Mickey. **I'd only feel...cheap.**

<u>SCENE 10. EXT. THE SKY. NIGHT.</u>
(<u>The Jumbo Jet continues towards its doom, peacefully breasting</u>
<u>the clouds. **Mix to calendar. The days of the week are blown off:**</u>
<u>'MONDAY...TUESDAY...WEDNESDAY...' Then the months of the year:</u>
<u>'OCTOBER...NOVEMBER...DECEMBER...' Then the years:</u>
<u>'1940...1941...1942...' and so on. This takes some time.</u>)

<u>SCENE 11. INT. DR BIG'S CASTLE. NIGHT.</u>

DR BIG (<u>impatiently</u>): Why is this plane taking so long to reach the Small Forester's Hut? I have been waiting literally ages. I

must shout at somebody over the telephone.

(He seizes a phone and gets a long distance number by dialling a

mere two digits. The person at the other end answers

immediately.)

DR BIG: Look, how will I be able to shoot the plane down so that

it lands on that awful show they are playing tonight - and so

dominate the known world?

(Without waiting for a reply, Dr Big slams the receiver down)

DR BIG: Pah!

SIDE-KICK: Fire mountain say you have broken our island taboo!

DR BIG: Side-Kick, you are fired! Or rather you will be fired -

at the Jumbo Jet! Ah ha! After that, even your best friends

won't know you!

(Other assistants scramble to do Dr Big's bidding)

DR BIG: Don't do that. That's my bidding.

SCENE 12. EXT. ANOTHER PART OF THE FOREST. NIGHT.

(A passing actor with a large part hoves into view. He is either

Roger Moore or Alec Guinness or whoever happens to be available.

He is, however, British and, thus, the music score breaks into

'Land of Hope and Glory'. As he wanders through the forest we

catch glimpses of Buckingham Palace, Piccadilly Circus, Trafalgar

Square, the Tower of London, but not in any logical order. The

Passing Actor is accompanied by another British actor - this one

with a small part - whose name one has never quite managed to

remember (played by Sam Kydd).

PASSING ACTOR (<u>nervously</u>): I don't like it.

OTHER ACTOR: No, but the Special Effects are good.

PASSING ACTOR: OK., **you keep him busy. I'll work round behind him.**

OTHER ACTOR: Who d'you mean?

PASSING ACTOR: Dr Big, of course.

OTHER ACTOR: I've got a better idea. Let's turn on the radio and see whether war has been declared. (<u>He does so. **Immediately the old set warms up.**</u>)

VOICE ON RADIO: 'War has been declared. A statement issued by the Government at three o'clock this afternoon stated...'

(<u>The OTHER ACTOR **turns off the radio without listening to any more** of the</u> broadcast.)

OTHER ACTOR: That clinches it. If we let Lassie free, **he's sure to lead us to Dr Big.**

LASSIE (<u>actually it's a she this time</u>): Woof!

PASSING ACTOR: Good idea. But we'd better act quickly. In fact, we'd better act a bit better than we are at the moment. I have a feeling there isn't much time left and something awful is about to happen...

<u>SCENE 13. INT. DR BIG'S CASTLE. NIGHT.</u>
(<u>A large gun, loaded with Side-Kick, is pointing at the sky. Dr Big is instructing one of his Chinese assisants to do his bidding in language the assistant will understand</u>)

DR BIG: So, lewember, **you're going to thlow the flight in round tlwo!**[4]

---

[4] Translation: 'You're going to throw the fight in round two.'

CHINESE: In that case, if caught, I shall have to say 'I voss only obeying orders'!

DR BIG: Ah ha! (to camera) You see, we have ways and means of making them talk![5]

SCENE 14. INT. THE SMALL FORESTER'S HUT. NIGHT.
(The Vicomte and His Intended are proudly watching Mickey Rooney and Judy Garland perform on stage. At first it had seemed as though Judy Garland might go out as a star and come back as a youngster, but this impression has since been corrected.)

SCENE 15. EXT. THE SKY. NIGHT.
(The Jumbo Jet is nearing the airspace above the Small Forester's Hut and Dr Big's Castle, looking understandably rather weary. Caption: 'Meanwhile, back at the ranch...'

SCENE 16. INT. DR BIG'S CASTLE. NIGHT.

DR BIG: Fire!

SCENE 17. EXT. THE SKY. NIGHT.
(The Jumbo jet is hit by Side-Kick, falls from the sky, narrowly misses the Small Forester's Hut, and buries itself in a snowdrift. A lot of material has to be got through here: several passengers have to die in slow motion; the Cowardly Passenger has to prove that he's really a hero; a person who narrowly missed flying on the crashed plane has to be rather relieved; we have to be shown

[5] Noted buff, L. Halliwell, tells us that perhaps the first film this line was used in was *Lives of a Bengal Lancer* (1935). Douglas Dumbrille as the evil Mohammed Khan says 'We have ways of making men talk.'

children's toys in the wreckage while our hearts are plucked; and, of course, one of the crew members has to go back into the inferno (or earthquake, if preferred) to rescue a tiny kitten which goes meow, meow. 'When all this is out of the way, we can get on with.)

SCENE 18. EXT. ANOTHER PART OF THE FOREST. NIGHT.

PASSING ACTOR: Good Lord, did you see what I saw?
OTHER ACTOR: Yes, what <u>was</u> the name of the bloke who played the Cowardly Passenger?
PASSING ACTOR: We must get to Dr Big's Castle without delay. Taxi!

(A taxi magically appears from nowhere. It is spotlessly clean.)

PASSING ACTOR: Follow that van!
SID JAMES: Sorry, guv. It's not going my way.
PASSING ACTOR (<u>taken back</u>): I don't usually have this trouble calling cabs in movies...

SCENE 19. INT. A VERY BIG SCENE. NIGHT.

(The Passing Actor's taxi draws up. He pays the driver without having any problems over change.)

PASSING ACTOR (breathlessly pointing at Dr Big who is being kept at bay by Lassie): Arrest that man!
LASSIE: Woof, woof!

(Dr Big pulls a small pistol out of his unspecified artificial limb - which has tight leather covering - and threatens to shoot the dog.)

JUDY GARLAND (<u>flushed with her triumph</u>): Oh, please, Dr Big,
don't shoot my dog! Lassie <u>couldn't</u> have killed those sheep!

MICKEY ROONEY (<u>to The Vicomte</u>): Gee, why can't I make you see
I've got music inside of me, Pa?

THE VICOMTE: After <u>that</u> performance?!

PASSING ACTOR: Excuse me, Monsieur Le Vicomte, I have now one or
two rather tedious speeches to make summing up what has been going
on, O K ?

THE VICOMTE: Oh, go right ahead. **But tell me, Inspector, how did
you know it was Dr Big?**

PASSING ACTOR: **Simple, really.** For a start, (<u>pointing at Mickey
Rooney</u>) that is not your son, Vicomte. That is your daughter.
(<u>Sensation</u>) Number two, the unfortunate Side-Kick who was fired
missile-style at the Jumbo Jet was none other than the great
songwriter Franz Schubert who was about to compose a little number
entitled 'Gilly Gilly Ossenfeffer Katzenellen Bogen By The Sea'.

OTHER ACTOR: **I think Schubert ought to leave songwriting alone.**

HIS INTENDED: But, Inspector, who is the evil Chinese assistant
who fired Franz Schubert, alias Side-Kick, at the Jumbo Jet?

PASSING ACTOR: It is my belief that he is not Chinese at all, but
the sinister international Mastermind and quiz show chairman,
Magnus Magnusson!

TUTTI: Gasp!

POSSE: **No trial for us. We're for stringing him up right away.**

THE VICOMTE: Which only leaves us with Dr Big. Who <u>is</u> he,
Inspector?

PASSING ACTOR: I will need some help from my colleague before I
can answer that question, Vicomte. (<u>To Other Actor:</u>) Who <u>is</u> this
evil killer, also known as Dr Big?

OTHER ACTOR: **The killer's name, Inspector, is...aaaagggghhhh!!!**

(<u>Collapses</u>)

PASSING ACTOR (<u>without batting an eyelid</u>): Quite so! The

killer's name is '...aaaagggghhhh!!!' A bit peculiar, I agree,

but there you go.

THE VICOMTE: So, all's well that end's well! But before we roll

the final credits, there's...

(He goes to the door and turns)

Just one more thing...

(Mickey Rooney and Judy Garland <u>rush towards each other in slow</u>

<u>motion to embrace. The Vicomte and His Intended sink slowly in</u>

<u>the West. And the Passing Actor and the Other Actor drive off</u>

<u>into the sunset.</u>)

THE END.

*

Two Can Play At This Game

Since that script was written there has only been one major cliché innovation from Hollywood. It has nothing to do with what appears on the screen but affects the titles of films. Nowadays, it is best to disregard titles including the following phrases:

> Son of ...
> The Return Of ...
> —— Revisited
> —— Strikes Again
> The Revenge of ...

Instead, all sequels should be numbered 2 or II (*Jaws 2, The French Connection II, Friday the Thirteenth Part II, Rocky 38* etc.) However, there is no news yet of one anticipated sequel: *Timbuk 2*.

Up The Orinoco With Torch And Pen

If you don't think you are quite made out for a career in the movies, then why not try your hand at being a critic? No experience is necessary, but here are one or two tips to help you on your way:

1) D. Powell, distinguished film critic and doyenne, suggests you use the word **enigmatic** as frequently as possible – as in, 'M. Antonioni's enigmatic new masterpiece, *The Passenger*.' This is a polite way of saying you haven't a clue what he's on about.

(Incidentally, Miss Powell always arrives at press previews a few minutes after the film has begun. A nice thought. This is so as not to disappoint her readers by giving away the start of the movie.)

2) Never mind if you haven't seen all a director's previous films – just one will do. Then you can say that the new film is **not as good as his earlier work**. It is also very important that you stand up and be counted from time to time and say things like: 'This latest picture, *The Subtitles*, proves conclusively that Paul Pseudlitz is **the most underrated** director working in the cinema today.'

Slogans Almost Write Themselves

If even the critic's job seems beyond your capabilities you might be able to manage to compose the slogans with which films are promoted. These almost write themselves: '**He was a werewolf, she was** a virgin of sixteen ... plus **cast of thousands ... a savage story of lust and ambition**[1] ...' and so on.

Remember that there is a lot of genius about in the movies but it should always be referred to backwards. An advertisement for some old Alfred Hitchcock films shown in London (November 1983) ran thus:

> 'This is a unique opportunity to see these classic films and either re-live or experience for the first time **the genius that is Hitchcock**.'

[1] As used, for example, to promote *Room At The Top* (1958).

However, beware of using **The Movie They Said Could Never Be Made**. As you can see from the above script, it already has, in one way or another.

My Cliché And I

... so, I suppose, she is entitled to do whatever she likes with it. We, her loyal subjects, can but follow her example. If, when opening the Barbican Centre in March 1982, Her Majesty finds the Royal speech-writer telling her to say **at the end of the day** ... then we can only assume that she and he, as grown people, know what they are doing.

Her Majesty, probably wisely, had discontinued use of her most famous cliché **my husband and I.** This featured in many of her top-rated Christmas broadcasts for several years and became almost as famous as her **God bless your awl** which, happily, she still continues to use. It is a lesson we should all digest that, from time to time, it is a good thing to rest some of our best clichés. When we reintroduce them at a later date they have so much more freshness.

It is not given to very many of us to be members of the Royal Family and to go around chatting to people, unveiling plaques, waving, and so on. However, should **one** ever find **one's self** in this enviable position **one** should note two very handy phrases:

1) **How very interesting**
   (this should be spoken in a flat, even tone, without emotion.)
2) **You must have seen a lot of changes in your time?**
   (ditto.)

And always remember:

The Royal family is not in a position to answer back.

For most of us, though, the nearest we are ever likely to get to the throne is through the perceptive comments of such observers as T. Fleming. Mr Fleming has assumed the mantle of BBC Television's Royal Microphone-in-Waiting previously worn by R. Dimbleby (though presumably the mantle had to be taken in a touch.)

At the wedding of Prince Charles, the Royal Father-in-Waiting, and Her Royal Fairy-Tale the Pregnancy of Wales, on 29 July 1981, T. Fleming excelled himself. He knew, for example, that royal brides should always be described as **like a fairy-tale princess** and/or the more usual **radiant** even when, as in the case of Her Royal Handbag, the P. Anne, in 1973, this took considerable nerve to say. T. Fleming began his commentary with **Once upon a time** ... – a pleasant touch – and made reference to **'the time-honoured ritual of a British royal occasion'**. What a pity that **Long may she reign** and ... **Glorious Years** had to be held over till another occasion.

Thank You, Archbishop

Full marks to R. Runcie, Archbishop of Canterbury and pig-breeder, for picking up on all this and beginning his address in St Paul's with: **Here is the stuff of which fairy tales are made.**

That's the stuff, Your Grace!

May The Words Of My Lips ...

... and the meditation of our hearts be ever acceptable in thy sight, O Lord! Amen.

The Sardine Principle

A. Bennett said it all. In a brilliant sketch for the revue *Beyond The Fringe* (1961) he devised – quite by chance, I'm sure – an Anglican sermon which, I know, has been played over and studied at many theological colleges. Its message and style have clearly been taken to heart by clergymen of many denominations, judging by their efforts today. I would just mention three of the key phrases for Christian sermonizers:

after quoting a biblical text, describe them as:
> **words very meaningful and significant for us gathered together tonight**

next, add:
> **perhaps I could say the same thing in a different way ...**

and then say:
> **life, you know, is ...** ('rather like opening a tin of sardines' etc.)

Building on Alan's example ('in a loud voice', as it says in the Book of Common Prayer), you might care to practise your own bit of uplift in front of the bathroom mirror.

Priestland's Progress

However, it should be emphasized that you do not have to wear a dog-collar to indulge in this sort of thing. You can do it in a pork-pie hat! CAC member, the Rt Revd David

Cyril-Lord, former Bishop of Basingstoke, is very keen on the work of inspirational religious broadcaster G. Priestland. I agree. That fellow has just the right sort of voice for this sort of thing and quite clearly is tall enough to be a bishop himself. So, let's take some advice from a professional communicator ...

The Cliché Advisory Committee was privileged to watch a re-play of a video called *Priestland Right And Wrong* (first broadcast on Channel 4 in 1983). They were ecstatic in their reception of such Priestlandisms as the following (which so cleverly blend religious clichés with those from the real world):

> ... in Christian terms
> if you'll excuse the pun
> pun intended!!
> ... of yesteryear
> in our society
> the game of Life
> the purpose of Life
> vultures coming home to roost
> speaking of a Brave New World
> a way of finding God's will for us
> a framework for spiritual growth
> trampling on human dignity
> green and pleasant land
> who did very nicely out of it, thank you

The Parable Of The Bishop And The Actress
Unfortunately, the CAC did not consider this relevant and so it has been excluded.

Superb Estate Agent To Let

People often poke fun at estate agents. Well, when they have names like Gascoigne-Pees and Doolittle and Dalley, that's not so surprising, is it? But estate agents have a very boring job to do and only get a measly two or three per cent commission out of sales worth tens of thousands of pounds. So be reasonable.

Selling Your House

The chief thing about writing estate agents' advertisements is to realize that their language includes built-in inflation. So, if you want to say a property is:

'ordinary', you should write:
   luxury
'all right'
   superb
'OK'
   magnificent
'half-an-hour from the station'
   within a few minutes walking distance of the station
'a mess'
   has possibilities
'neither one thing nor the other'
   maisonette
'small'
   bijou residence
'up for sale'
   unique opportunity
'still standing'
   well looked after

'not next to a gas holder'
   in a pleasant position
'handy for the railway station' (i.e. overlooking the goods yards):
   ideally situated
'anywhere'
   in one of the finest areas
'not in a rubbish dump'
   has a landscaped front garden
'cheap'
   ideal for first-time buyer
'pokey'
   in a small exclusive development
'off the beaten track'
   in a quiet and mature locality
'in a cul-de-sac'
   in a long-established character road
'rip-off'
   select development
'available' or 'sticking'
   sought after
'not as small as it looks'
   deceptively   spacious (*not* 'deceptively cramped'!)

I happily pass on the wonder-job that was done on a completely derelict property just down the road from where I live. It was billed as:
   offering enormous potential for improvement

PS If in any doubt, put up the price.

In A Packed Programme Tonight

The cliché connoisseur is drawn irresistibly towards the spoken meeja. Whenever he flicks on that radio or television switch, he finds a veritable pot-pourri. Here then, for programme-makers, meeja figures, viewers and listeners alike, is a spotter's guide to broadcast clichés. It is based on my occasional, informal coaching classes for BBC, ITV and ILR staff, lispingly known as the Reith lectures. These have been supplemented by useful conversations with CAC member Mike Kevin, formerly of BBC Radio Bootle and now with ITN.

The Cliché In Radio And Television
I always begin my sessions by quoting the little child – or was it *Radio Times* correspondent? – who commented: 'I like wireless more than television **because the pictures are so much better.'** This quotation is mandatory in all discussions of broadcasting.

Other points well-worth making in this context are: **British television is the best in the world** and **television is killing the art of conversation.** When discussing TV news, it is essential to make reference to **the ancient habit of killing messengers who bring bad news.** When accused of manslaughter you should say, 'I did it **because I'd just been watching** *Play for Today.'*

But let us get on to the programmes themselves:

Choosing A Signature Tune
You must have a good 'sig. tune', as they call it in the trade. The best you can possibly have is **'Fanfare for the Common Man'** played by Emerson, Lake and Palmer. In 1983, some

five programmes on British TV and radio were using it. On one occasion, two of the TV programmes were shown consecutively, but no one seemed to mind.

Choosing A Title

A good title is as essential as a catchy sig. tune. You are advised to avoid the 1960s penchant for long titles, such as *That Was The Week That Was* and *Not So Much A Programme More A Way Of Life*, as these tend to get shortened anyway. Go for something more immediately punchy. Useful formats are:

A **Question** of ... (Sport, Confidence, Stars, Politics, Degree etc. cf. *The Body in Question*)

... **Rules OK** (as in Town Hall, Queen Elizabeth etc.)

The ... Programme (as in Book, Money, Food, So-Called etc.)

... **'85** (as in Film, Decision, Election etc.)

Promoting Your Programme In Radio Times *Or* TV Times
You should never claim that there is anything of a satirical nature in your programme. The word 'satire' has been banned since 1963. Any breach of this rule can lead to questions being asked in Parliament and stacks of letters from loony listeners. The correct phrases to use are:

a **light-hearted look at** ...
a **sideways glance at** ...
a **tongue-in-cheek look at** ...
an **irreverent look back at** ...
a **quizzical look at** ...

or any combination of these, as in 'an irreverent tongue-in-cheek sideways glance at the week's news'.

When a programme is repeated, on no account should the word 'repeat' be used. The correct expressions are: **another chance to see** ... and **in response to many requests, a special showing of** ...

All magazine programmes must be described as

containing **news, views and interviews**.

Promoting Your Programme On The Air

Those little cracks between programmes not filled with advertisements are useful for noting forthcoming attractions. In the BBC these are known as 'trails' (i.e. trailers) and in ITV 'promos' (short for 'promotion spots'). Making them is something of a chore, as they often take longer to prepare than the actual programmes. This should not put you off. Many more people will see the trails than the programmes.

Serious programmes should promise to 'look behind' things, as this is very popular. For example, Arthur Negus might say: 'In this week's programme **we look behind** eighteenth century commodes.'

Equally successful is the 'we ask' method. For example: 'In tonight's editions of *Panorama* **we ask** – is there a future for the one-legged trouser?' This can usefully be extended when you have prepared a film report which is not strictly relevant to the piece of news you wish to 'peg' it to. Hence: **'And as** the Labour Party gathers for its conference at Brighton, *Newsnight* **asks** why the Militant Tendency is heading for Moscow?

Useful alternatives to this are **on the eve of ... we ask** and headlines containing 'Also' with 'Or' questions, viz. **'Also:** Barbara Cartland: National Treasure or White Elephant?'

These approaches should not cause you to forget asking 'Who is the real ...?' – as in: **'Who is the real** Norman Krebs?' (always assuming of course that there is one).

If W. Shakespeare, playwright and **Bard of Avon**, had been employed writing programme trails, he would probably have come up with something like this:

> 'To be, or not to be ... **that is the question to which we devote the whole of this week's** *Panorama*. Whether it is nobler in the mind to suffer the slings and arrows of outrageous fortune or to take arms against a sea of troubles

– the Defence Secretary **faces tough questioning from** a leading psychiatrist.

'And **we'll be asking** *him* what dreams may come when we have shuffled off this mortal coil.

'**We'll also have the first film** out of that undiscover'd country from whose bourne Richard Lindley reports.

'Later, there's a consummation devoutly to be wished with **a choice of viewing** on BBC Television which makes us rather bear those ills we have than fly to others that we know not of.

'For who would bear the whips and scorns of time? Well, **we sent** Monty Modlyn **to find out**. And in *Panorama*, tonight at ten past eight, **you can see what happened** to his bare bodkin …'

Light-hearted programmes are best summarized briefly before promising **all this – and more –** in …

What To Say When Planning Your Programme

Let's find out what the man-in-the-street wants to know/really thinks and **Let's put it in the language that the man-in-the-street will be able to understand**. Never reflect after the programme whether you have actually done any of these things. **You are only as good as your last programme.**

What To Say In The Studio Just Before You Go On The Air

'Good luck, everyone. Don't think of it as a quiz/epilogue/ farming programme – **just have fun, enjoy yourselves.**'

Opening And Closing Your Programme

All programmes (except plays) should begin with a 'menu' – headlines which tell you **what's coming up in the next half-hour** …, as when the presenter (smiling) says:

'Hello! **Later in the programme,** we'll be talking to wizard of the dribble, Lenny Snot, about his latest marriage, we'll be getting some tips on the kind of ducks you can have flying up your wall this Autumn, and we'll be hearing about the Jersey cow that *can't* play Beethoven's Sixth on a xylophone ...

'But first, (*suddenly adopting serious look*) the tragic news just in from Beirut/Belfast/Biggleswade ...'

A small variation: **More on that in a moment, but first ...**

If your programme follows a news bulletin and contains a continuation of one of the stories, you must bear in mind the listener or viewer who has just tuned in and does not know what you are talking about. Even if the street-fighting in Karachi was mentioned in the headlines of the bulletin, in the body of the bulletin, and in the re-cap at the end of the bulletin, you must always say: '**As you may have heard in the news,** street-fighting has broken out in Karachi.'

If your programme is devoted to news and current affairs and a particular story is trundling along, you must nevertheless always say: **We will, of course, bring you news of any further developments just as soon as they occur.** This should not sound like a threat, although there is the implicit promise that you will bring news of further developments even if they *don't* occur.

All programmes should end: 'Well, **I'm afraid that's all we have time for** this week. Next week ... till then, from all of us here, goodbye.' If you are a weather-forecaster, you are allowed to say, simply: **And, that's it!**

Things Disc Jockeys Should Say

1) Anybody who is dead and whose records still get played is, naturally, styled as: **The late, great ...**

2) Anybody who is not dead but has been around longer than two weeks is: 'Looking undeniably older but **sounding just as good as ever.**'

3) Anybody who can sing *and* play the piano is **multi-talented.**

4) Never say: 'There's a new record out today from Johnny Mathis, and I'll be playing you that record in just a

moment.' Always say: 'I'll be playing that **particular** record in just a moment.'

5) In fact, don't refer to records as such at all. **All the latest sounds around** are what you are playing.

Things Presenters Should Say

1) Anybody you have heard of and are slightly in awe of – without being terribly sure what it is they are famous for – must be introduced as **the distinguished** ... (e.g. 'Sir John Gielgud, the distinguished actor knight'). However, politicians may only be called 'distinguished' if they have retired, are in the House of Lords, or are foreign – in which case, they are probably 'distinguished statesmen' into the bargain.

2) The next step up the ladder is to call someone a **living legend** or a **legend in his own lifetime**. (This use is not restricted to broadcasting. M. Thatcher said of Speaker G. Thomas on his retirement from the House of Commons in May 1983): 'A great many have occupied your chair but it is a measure of your Speakership that you have become a legend in your lifetime.')

3) A very useful expression these days is **and who doesn't these days?** It does not have to make sense in any context but its purpose is to make the listener or viewer feel you are one of them. A more direct way of achieving this relationship with the viewer is to say **that's you and me** – as in, 'The Chancellor of the Exchequer today imposed a swingeing new tax on everybody who ever downed a well-earned pint, put a pony on a gee-gee, or lit up a Christmas cigar – that's you and me.'

Putting these two approaches together, you get something like this: 'Mrs Elsie Scroggins, like many another tax-payer – that's you and me – has been having periodic back-pains – and who doesn't these days? – but hers were back-pains with a difference ...'

4) Ah, yes, there goes another one: **with a difference**. Another example: 'On Sunday there is to be a sponsored pub crawl with a difference.' (I heard that on Radio Clyde,

but I can't remember what the difference was, unfortunately.)
5) A handy little gadget is the suffix – **style**. Instead of saying 'Like Pope John Paul II' say 'Pope John Paul II-style' and see where that gets you. This usage is now OK for use by Shakespeare-style wordsmiths.

Things Newscasters Should Say
When introducing film reports you have a choice of phrases:

a) 'When President Reagan opened his mouth, **our reporter**, Mike Kevin, **was there** ...'

b) 'Washington was stunned today when President Reagan opened his mouth. Mike Kevin **has that story** ...'

c) 'I'm rather worried that we may have lost that report by Mike Kevin but I'm told it's OK and I am now trying to hit my cue by saying Mike Kevin *now* **reports** ...'

Things Reporters Should Say
There is only one thing reporters should say viz.: **even as I speak** ... (as in, 'Even as I speak, there are a lot of wallies standing behind me making rude gestures at the camera.') There is absolutely no point in sending a reporter to stand on the spot somewhere if he does not say this. Otherwise he might just as well have stayed in the studio and saved us all a lot of money. Also useful: **time will tell.**

Things To Do While You Are Talking On TV
1) Walk slowly towards the camera **using your hands a lot.**
2) **Hold a silly microphone.**
3) Drive a car and **talk sideways to the camera.**
4) **Walk along talking sideways** to the camera, not looking where you are going.
5) Stand in the middle of nowhere **with your arms folded, nodding at people.**

Interviewing For Magazine And Chat Shows

The business of asking questions is not quite as easy as it looks but the following hints should see you through. You are strongly advised to say things like **I see from the cuttings that** ... and 'Mr Mitchum, **tell us the anecdote** about the brawl you got involved in at Shanghai,' as this shows you have done your homework. These questions are better than ones beginning **Didn't you once ...?** as this approach may reveal that the interviewee doesn't know what you think he knows and *you* will end up having to tell *him* his story.

Actors and actresses, particularly the more illustrious ones, should always be asked: **Do you still get nervous before a first night?** and '**What particular problems have you had** (playing Quasimodo, Raquel Welch?)'

Remember also: **Do you prefer acting in films to the live theatre/the live theatre to television/television to radio?** and '**Was** (the sugar-daddy who got you your first role) **a great influence on your career?**'

Anybody who is not a mere viewer can be asked: **What effect has fame had on your private life?**

Without fail, authors should be asked **How long did it take you to write this book?** (NB You may need a follow-up question quite soon after this as authors, being difficult people, may well throw a fit.) Also ask them: **How do you do all the research for your books?** and **Where do you get your ideas from?** However, this last question should not be put to T. Stoppard, playwright and Bard of Slough, as he is quite likely to reply, 'If I knew, I'd go there.'

A useful concluding question that you can ask anybody is: 'Well, **where do you go from here?**'

Interviewing For News Programmes

Only one question is necessary – **How did you feel ..?** as in, 'How did you feel when your daughter was raped/your house was blown up by the Gas Board/you discovered you'd forgotten to post the pools coupon and lost your next door neighbour one million pounds?'

On the other hand, if you really must ask another question, do not forget: **Just how serious** ... as in 'Just how serious is the gangrene that is plaguing the rotten core of our inner cities?' Cliché connoisseur, M. Leapman, long ago recommended that the correct pronunciation for this should be 'justow-serious'.

Interviewing for Current Affairs Programmes

By way of introduction to this section, I should say that it is possible to conduct such interviews on radio and televison *without* using clichés. I have devised an all-purpose set of questions that will see you through any conventional interview, whatever the subject. The set will work even if you do not know to whom you are putting the questions or why you are doing so (I have used it on several such occasions myself and can vouch for its efficiency.) Here it is:

1) 'What's this all about then?'
2) 'Why has this happened now?'
3) 'So, what's going to happen next, d'you think?'

If this fails to fill up the allotted time, you can always fall back on the supplementary:

4) 'Do you *really* think that?'

This will keep any self-respecting pundit going for another minute, even if he is simply re-arranging words and thoughts he has already spoken – but more carefully than first time round.

The above format should only be used in emergencies, however. It is much better to spend time preparing your questions, thus ensuring the inclusion of the following:

> **I put it to you** – as in, 'Mr Scargill, I put it to you that, at times, it could be said you are a little less than in favour of wholesale pit closures?' This sounds tough but has the merit of avoiding nasty scenes in the hospitality room afterwards.

How would you answer those people who would say or **Some people would say** – as in, 'Some people would say, Prime Minister, that you are a devious bastard, permanently a-swill with brandy, and not caring a tinker's cuss for the plight of six million unemployed. What would you say to that?' This helps distance you, the interviewer, from the criticism while making sure you reflect it. If, even so, the Prime Minister in question should say 'I *am* surprised at you, *Mr* Day, asking a question like that,' you must respond with the formula: 'Of course, Prime Minister, I am merely reflecting **the sort of question people at home are probably asking** ...' You might just get away with it.

Briefly Be careful with this word (as in, 'Briefly, A.J.P. Taylor, what do you see as the future of Western Civilization?'). The viewer knows, the interviewee knows, and you know, that you are only saying this because you want the boring old buffer to give you a snappy answer to your final question. Even though people in the studio may be waving their arms about, foaming at the mouth or jumping up and down on their scripts, you may have given the interviewee a chance to sink you completely by rambling on and on, ruining the timing of the show. For this reason, you are ill-advised ever to say **'In two words**, Mr Chernenko, will there be war?' Few people can give two word answers or, if they can, they are usually not broadcastable.

I'm afraid we've run right out of time and **There we must leave it, I'm afraid**. If you cock up the timing completely, you'll just have to use one of these.

And that's about 'it' for this week, so until next week, from me, it's 'Goodbye'. (Gather papers together. Put pen back in pocket.)

His Death Diminishes Us All

Understandably, we all get tongue-tied when talking about death. Dying, funerals, bereavement and condolence are difficult matters. But, don't despair, there is a solution. Clichés. The first funeral I ever went to was a sparsely-attended affair at a crematorium. A cracked record of 'The Lord is My Shepherd' was used to supplement our hymn-singing and the minister Uriah-Heeped his way through the service. When we returned for the wake, one of the dear departed's contemporaries sighed deeply and declared to all and sundry: 'Well, that's **another page turned in the Book of Life!**'

Another Page Turned In The Book Of Life

That's the spirit! Funerals can be fun. Don't just embrace euphemisms. Use clichés and enjoy yourself. Should you be called upon to say a few words about the departed, you are bound to find something in the following funeral oration.

I myself composed it when David Kintlesham died in 1979. His memorial service was, of course, held at St James's, Piccadilly (Manchester). The sun shone brightly through the stained glass on a cold January morning as I climbed the polished marble steps and stood in the pulpit. The church was full of friends and relatives of the dear departed. I could hardly take my eyes off Daphne Kintlesham, however. She took it like a brick. This is what I said:

My Address At Lord Kintlesham's Memorial Service

'We are **gathered together today to remember the life of** Lord Kintlesham of Blundellsands.

'The death of David Kintlesham has **plucked from our midst,** in a very real sense, **one of the greatest and most significant figures in** the politics of the second half of the twentieth century, not forgetting Taiwanese lentils.

'The loss will be the more keenly felt by those who knew him. And **our hearts go out** to his wife, Daphne, in her **great sorrow.**

'**His death diminishes us all.** The more so, since he has been **taken from us** when he had **everything to live for.**

'One thing is certain: **he was a big man in every sense of the word,** also **he was a giant among men.** The other thing is that **his time had run out.**

'**I think above all he will be remembered as a** great fighter for truth.

'He was **approaching the summit of his achievement** or, as some would say, the **pinnacle of his endeavour** ... **but it was not to be.**

'It is some comfort, therefore, to know that **his work will live on.** Indeed, **his legend will live for ever.**

'He has **paid the supreme sacrifice** on behalf of the **land he loved so well – ah, the pity of it!**

'Today, there is a **lump in all our throats,** a **tugging at our heart strings,** and a **gaping hole in all our lives.**

'David's death marks the end of an era because when they made David Kintlesham they threw away the mould.

'A light has gone out in all our lives and we are all the poorer for his passing.

'Now, shortly, we will commit his mortal remains and, indeed, all that was mortal of him to the earth from which he came – and to which we must all one day return.

'So let me say, finally, that he was unique, he was a genius, and – in a very real sense – he is dead. He will be sadly missed and I think I can say we shall not see his like again.'

At The End Of The Day

A Final Word To The Reader

It is time to stop putting clichés **in bold print**. From now on you are capable of recognizing them for what they are. In the last analysis and when the chips are down, it is up to you to go forward, alone, into the Brave New World of clichés. Your parents didn't fight through two World Wars to create a quality of life barren of clichés. That was clearly not what it was all about. What ordinary folk – that's you and me – are after is like a dream come true. Only clichés can provide this. Without clichés life is totally unacceptable.

If you take the lessons of this book to heart, it will open up a whole new ball-game to you. And I don't mean maybe.

The members of the Cliché Advisory Council join me in wishing you every good wish in your endeavours.

Poem

THE JOY OF CLICHÉS

Tell me, what is the joy that you speak of?
  Do we know it, in this day and age?
Is there light at the end of the tunnel
  A chortle on every page?

At this moment in time, in the meeja,
  We Can Now Reveal, helped by our muse,
We're exposing the Shame Of Our Cities
  – As you may have just heard on the news.

Was your face red – or sick as a parrot –
  On that island of sun, sand and sea?
No mistake, it's the Scoop of the Century,

– If in doubt, please consult your GP.

In The Place They Are Calling Gomorrah
   The Press tries to print news that fits,
If our newshound's a Man For All Seasons,
   Believe me ... it's worse than the blitz.

In a house quite deceptively spacious
   As his wife and his family stand by
A Peer to the far right of Genghis
   Admits he's been living a lie.

'Every dream can turn into a nightmare,'
   SAYS SEX-GIRL ON MYSTERY TOUR,
'Every journey's a flight out of danger ...'
   (That is, sadly, all there's time for.)

At the end of the day, it takes genius –
   The Genius That's ... Lionel Blair –
To write, and make love, like a stallion,
   Yes, a talent that's *extraordinaire*!

For winning's the name of the game here –
   I agree – and who doesn't these days?
Alarm bells are ringing in Clapham ...
   Ah, such is the Joy of Clichés!

All Futura Books are available at your bookshop or
newsagent, or can be ordered from the following address:
Futura Books, Cash Sales Department,
P.O. Box 11, Falmouth, Cornwall.

Please send cheque or postal order (no currency), and
allow 55p for postage and packing for the first book
plus 22p for the second book and 14p for each additional
book ordered up to a maximum charge of £1.75 in U.K.

Customers in Eire and B.F.P.O. please allow 55p for
the first book, 22p for the second book plus 14p per
copy for the next 7 books, thereafter 8p per book.

Overseas customers please allow £1 for postage and
packing for the first book and 25p per copy for each
additional book.